CALCULUS
GRAPHICAL, NUMERICAL, ALGEBRAIC

ASSESSMENT

Prentice
Hall

Glenview, Illinois
Needham, Massachusetts
Upper Saddle River, New Jersey

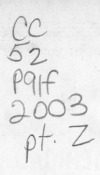

Introduction

This publication contains the following assessment materials to accompany
Calculus: Graphical, Numerical, Algebraic:

• Chapter Tests, Forms A and B
    Free-response, multiple choice
• Semester Tests, Forms A and B
    Free response, multiple choice
• Quizzes
    Covering 2-3 sections
• Chapter Alternative Assessment
    Group Activity, Student Log (or Journal), Discussion Question
• Chapter self-tests are available on the World Wide Web at **www.phschool.com.**

C O N T E N T S

1. Find the slope of the line determined by points $A(-1, 3)$ and $B(4, 7)$.

   (A) $\dfrac{3}{4}$ (B) $\dfrac{4}{3}$ (C) $\dfrac{4}{5}$ (D) $\dfrac{5}{4}$ (E) $-\dfrac{4}{5}$

1. _____

2. Find an equation for the line through the point $P(3, -2)$ that is perpendicular to the line $3x + 2y = 5$.

   (A) $y = -\dfrac{2}{3}x$ (B) $y = -\dfrac{3}{2}x + \dfrac{5}{2}$

   (C) $y = \dfrac{2}{3}x - 4$ (D) $y = \dfrac{3}{2}x - \dfrac{13}{2}$

   (E) $y = -\dfrac{5}{3}x + 3$

2. _____

3.

Age (weeks)	2	3	4	5	6
Weight (pounds)	4.2	6.3	7.1	9.2	10.5

The table shows the growth of a certain puppy. Find the linear regression equation for the data. Use the linear regression equation to estimate the weight of the puppy at age 8 weeks, rounded to the nearest pound.

   (A) 13 pounds   (B) 14 pounds   (C) 15 pounds
   (D) 16 pounds   (E) 17 pounds

3. _____

4. Which of the following is an odd function?

   (A) $y = (x - 5)^3$ (B) $y = 2 + |x|$ (C) $y = x^5 - \sqrt{x}$
   (D) $y = 2x^3 + 4x$ (E) $y = x^3 \cdot x^5$

4. _____

5. Draw the graph of the function.

$$f(x) = \begin{cases} -2, & x < -2 \\ x^2 - 2, & -2 \le x < 0 \\ x - 2, & x \ge 0 \end{cases}$$

5.

$[-4, 4]$ by $[-3, 3]$

6. Which of the following exponential expressions is equivalent to 25^{4x}?

   (A) 5^{6x} (B) 5^{8x} (C) 5^{10x} (D) 5^{12x} (E) 5^{14x}

6. _____

7. Use a graph to solve the equation $3^{-x} = 7$.

   (A) $x \approx -2.33$ (B) $x \approx -1.77$ (C) $x \approx 0.56$
   (D) $x \approx 1.77$ (E) $x \approx 2.33$

7. _____

1. Graph the parametrized curve given by $x = t - 2$, $y = -2 + \sqrt{5t}, 0 \le t \le 4$. Indicate the direction in which the curve is traced.

1.

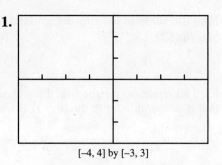

[–4, 4] by [–3, 3]

2. Find a Cartesian equation for a curve that contains the parametrized curve given by $x = t - 2, y = -2 + \sqrt{5t}, 0 \le t \le 4$.

2. _____

(A) $y = -2 + \sqrt{5x + 10}$ (B) $y = -2 + \sqrt{5x}$

(C) $y = -2 + \sqrt{5x - 10}$ (D) $y = -2 + \sqrt{x + 2}$

(E) $y = 2 - \sqrt{x + 2}$

3. For $f(x) = x^2 - 3, x \le 0$, find $f^{-1}(x)$.

3. _____

(A) $f^{-1}(x) = \sqrt{x + 2}$ (B) $f^{-1}(x) = -\sqrt{x + 3}$

(C) $f^{-1}(x) = \sqrt{x - 3}$ (D) $f^{-1}(x) = -\sqrt{x - 3}$

(E) $f^{-1}(x) = 3 - x$

4. Let $f(x) = e^{x - 1}, 0 \le x \le 3$. Which of the following is a parametrization for the graph of $y = f^{-1}(x)$?

4. _____

(A) $x = t, y = e^{t - 1}, 0 \le t \le 3$
(B) $x = t, y = 1 + \ln t, 0 \le t \le 3$
(C) $x = e^{t - 1}, y = t, 0 \le t \le 3$
(D) $x = 1 + \ln t, y = t, 0 \le t \le 3$
(E) $x = t, y = e^{1-t}, 0 \le t \le 3$

5. Solve the equation $4^x + 4^{-x} = \dfrac{5}{2}$ algebraically.

5. _____

(A) $x = \dfrac{1}{2}$ (B) $x = -\dfrac{1}{2}, x = \dfrac{1}{2}$

(C) $x = -1, x = 1$ (D) $x = -\dfrac{1}{2}, x = 0, x = \dfrac{1}{2}$

(E) $x = -1, x = 0, x = 1$

6. Solve the equation $\sec x = \sqrt{2}$ in the interval $0 \le x \le 2\pi$.

6. _____

(A) $x = -\dfrac{\pi}{4}, x = \dfrac{\pi}{4}$ (B) $x = \dfrac{\pi}{4}, x = \dfrac{3\pi}{4}$

(C) $x = \dfrac{\pi}{4}, x = \dfrac{5\pi}{4}$ (D) $x = \dfrac{3\pi}{4}, x = \dfrac{5\pi}{4}$

(E) $x = \dfrac{\pi}{4}, x = \dfrac{7\pi}{4}$

Directions: Show all steps leading to your answers, including any intermediate results obtained using a graphing utility. Use the back of the test or another sheet of paper if necessary.

1. Find the slope of the line determined by points $A(8, -2)$ and $B(2, 7)$.

    (A) $\frac{2}{3}$ (B) $-\frac{2}{3}$ (C) $\frac{3}{2}$ (D) $-\frac{3}{2}$ (E) -2

    1. _____

2. Let L represent the line $y = \frac{3}{5}x + 7$. Write an equation for the line through $P(6, -4)$ that is **(a)** parallel to L, **(b)** perpendicular to L.

    2. (a) _____
    (b) _____

3. For the function $y = 5 - \sqrt{9 - x^2}$, **(a)** find the domain, **(b)** find the range, and **(c)** determine whether the function is odd, even or neither.

    3. (a) _____
    (b) _____
    (c) _____

4. Let $f(x) = \begin{cases} -0.5x, & x < -2 \\ \sqrt{x + 2}, & x \geq -2 \end{cases}$.

    (a) Draw the graph of $f(x)$.

    (b) Find the domain.

    (c) Find the range.

    4. (a)

    [−4, 4] by [−3, 3]

    (b) _____
    (c) _____

5. Let $f(x) = x^2 + 5$ and $g(x) = \frac{1}{x}$.
    Find formulas for **(a)** $f \circ g$ and **(b)** $g \circ f$.

    5. (a) _____
    (b) _____

6. State the domain, range, and intercepts of the function $y = 2^{-x} - 1$.

    6. Domain: _____
    Range: _____
    x-intercept(s): _____
    y-intercept(s): _____

7. Use a graph to solve the equation $4 - 3^x = 0$.

    7. _____

8. Suppose that in any given year, the population of a certain endangered species is reduced by 25%. If the population is now 7500, in how many years will the population be 4000?

    8. _____

9. Find a parametrization for the left half of the parabola $y = x^2 - 4x + 3$.

    9. _____

NAME

10. **(a)** Graph the parametrized curve described by
$x = 2 \sin t$, $y = -3 \cos t$, $0 \le t \le \pi$. Indicate the
direction in which the curve is traced.

10. (a)

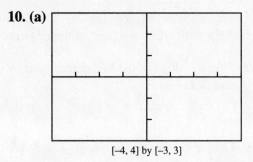

[−4, 4] by [−3, 3]

(b) Find a Cartesian equation for the parametrized curve.
What portion of the graph of the Cartesian equation
is traced by the parametrized curve?

(b) _____

_____

_____

11. Let $f(x) = \sqrt[3]{x + 2}$ and $g(x) = x^3 - 2$.
Which of the following are true?
I. $g(x) = f^{-1}(x)$ for all real values of x.
II. $(f \circ g)(x) = 1$ for all real values of x.
III. The function f is one-to-one.

(A) I and II (B) I and III (C) II and III
(D) III only (E) I, II, and III

11. _____

12. Let $f(x) = \sqrt{3 - x}$.
Find an expression for $f^{-1}(x)$.
(Be sure to state any necessary domain restrictions.)

12. _____

13. The table gives Taiwan's nuclear power generation
data in billions of kilowatt-hours. Let $x = 5$ represent
1980, $x = 10$ represent 1985, and so on.

13. (a) _____
(b) _____

Year	1980	1985	1990	1995
Energy produced	7.8	27.8	31.6	33.9

(a) Find a natural logarithm regression equation for
the data.

(b) Predict when Taiwan's nuclear power
generation will reach 40 billion kilowatt-hours.

14. An angle measuring $\dfrac{3\pi}{8}$ radians has its vertex at the center
of a circle whose radius is 4 feet. Find the length of the
subtended arc.

14. _____

15. Let $y = 3 \sin(2x - \pi) + 2$. Determine the period,
domain, and range of the function.

15. Period: _____

Domain: _____

Range: _____

16. Solve the equation $\cot x = 4$ in the interval $0 \le x \le 2\pi$.

16. _____

Directions: Show all steps leading to your answers, including any intermediate results obtained using a graphing utility. Use the back of the test or another sheet of paper if necessary.

1. Find the slope of the line determined by points $P(-3, 7)$ and $Q(1, 13)$.

   (A) $\frac{2}{3}$ (B) $-\frac{2}{3}$ (C) $\frac{3}{2}$ (D) $-\frac{3}{2}$ (E) -2

   1. _____

2. Let L represent the line $y = -\frac{4}{3}x + 2$. Write an equation for the line through $P(9, -7)$ that is (a) parallel to L, (b) perpendicular to L.

   2. (a) _____

   (b) _____

3. For the function $y = -2 + \sqrt{x^2 - 25}$, (a) find the domain, (b) find the range, and (c) determine whether the function is odd, even or neither.

   3. (a) _____

   (b) _____

   (c) _____

4. Let $f(x) = \begin{cases} \sqrt{1 - x}, & x \le 1 \\ 0.5x - 2, & x > 1 \end{cases}$

   (a) Draw the graph of $g(x)$.

   (b) Find the domain.

   (c) Find the range.

   4. (a)

   $[-4, 4]$ by $[-3, 3]$

   (b) _____

   (c) _____

5. Let $f(x) = \frac{1}{x - 2}$ and $g(x) = 5x^2$.
   Find formulas for (a) $f \circ g$ and (b) $g \circ f$.

   5. (a) _____

   (b) _____

6. State the domain, range, and intercepts of the function $y = 9 - 3^x$.

   6. Domain: _____
   Range: _____
   x-intercept(s): _____
   y-intercept(s): _____

7. Use a graph to solve the equation $2^{-x} - 6 = 0$.

   7. _____

8. Suppose that in any given year, the value of a certain investment is increased by 15%. If the value is now $15,000, in how many years will the value be $21,000?

   8. _____

9. Find a parametrization for the right half of the parabola $y = x^2 + 6x - 7$.

   9. _____

10. (a) Graph the parametrized curve described by $x = 2 \cos t$, $y = -\sin t$, $0 \le t \le \pi$. Indicate the direction in which the curve is traced.

10. (a)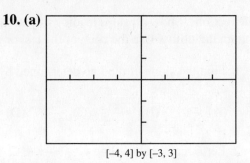

[-4, 4] by [-3, 3]

    (b) Find a Cartesian equation for the parametrized curve. What portion of the graph of the Cartesian equation is traced by the parametrized curve?

    (b) _____

_____

_____

11. Let $f(x) = \dfrac{1}{x^2 + 2}$, $x > 0$, and $g(x) = \sqrt{\dfrac{1}{x} - 2}$.

11. _____

Which of the following are true?

  I. $g(x) = f^{-1}(x)$ for all real values of x.

  II. $(g \circ f)(x) = x$ for all $x > 0$.

  III. The function f is one-to-one.

  (A) I and II   (B) I and III   (C) II and III

  (D) III only   (E) I, II, and III

12. Let $f(x) = -\sqrt{x + 5}$.

12. _____

Find an expression for $f^{-1}(x)$.
(Be sure to state any necessary domain restrictions.)

13. The table gives Sweden's nuclear power generation data in billions of kilowatt-hours. Let $x = 5$ represent 1980, $x = 10$ represent 1985, and so on.

13. (a) _____

    (b) _____

Year	1980	1985	1990	1995
Energy produced	25.3	55.8	65.2	66.5

    (a) Find a natural logarithm regression equation for the data.

    (b) Predict when Sweden's nuclear power generation will reach 85 billion kilowatt-hours.

14. An angle measuring $\dfrac{5\pi}{6}$ radians has its vertex at the center of a circle whose radius is 7 meters. Find the length of the subtended arc.

14. _____

15. Let $y = 5 \tan\left(x + \dfrac{\pi}{2}\right) - 3$. Determine the period, domain, and range of the function.

15. Period: _____

    Domain: _____

    Range: _____

16. Solve the equation $\sec x = -3$ in the interval $0 \le x \le 2\pi$.

16. _____

1. Determine $\lim\limits_{x \to 5} (2x^2 - 4x + 7)$ by substitution.
               1. _____

(A) 7   (B) 12   (C) 37   (D) 47   (E) 57

2. Find $\lim\limits_{x \to 2} \dfrac{x^2 + x - 6}{x - 2}$, if it exists.
           2. _____

(A) 0   (B) 3   (C) 5

(D) 6   (E) Does not exist

3. For the function $y = f(x)$ whose graph is shown below,
           3. _____

which statement is false?

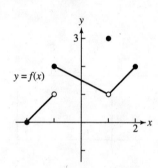

(A) $\lim\limits_{x \to 1} f(x) = 1$

(B) $\lim\limits_{x \to 2^-} f(x) = 2$

(C) $\lim\limits_{x \to 0^+} f(x) = \lim\limits_{x \to 0^-} f(x)$

(D) $\lim\limits_{x \to -1} f(x) = 2$

(E) $\lim\limits_{x \to -1^+} f(x) = 2$

4. Let $f(x) = \begin{cases} x^2 - 2, & x < 1 \\ -\dfrac{1}{2}x + 1, & x \geq 1 \end{cases}$. What is $\lim\limits_{x \to 1^+} f(x)$?
    4. _____

(A) -1 (B) $\dfrac{1}{2}$ (C) 1

(D) 1.73   (E) Does not exist

5. Find $\lim\limits_{x \to 3^+} \dfrac{x + 3}{x - 3}$
                    5. _____

(A) 0   (B) 6   (C) -6 (D) $-\infty$ (E) ∞

6. Which of the following is a horizontal asymptote for
    6. _____

$f(x) = \dfrac{6x^2 + 2x - 4}{2x^2 + 3x + 2}$?

(A) $y = -3$ (B) $y = -2$ (C) $y = 2$

(D) $y = 3$ (E) $y = 4$

7. Find $\lim\limits_{x \to -\infty} \dfrac{|8x + 6|}{4x - 2}$
                7. _____

(A) -3 (B) -2 (C) 2   (D) 3   (E) 4

8. Which of the following is a right end behavior model for
    8. _____

$y = x^3 - e^{-x}$?

(A) x^3 (B) $-e^{-x}$ (C) e^{-x} (D) e^x (E) $-x^3$

1. The function f whose graph is shown below is continuous
at which of the following points?

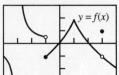

[–4, 4] by [–3, 3]

(A) $x = -3$ (B) $x = -1$ (C) $x = 1$
(D) $x = 3$ (E) All of these.

1. _____

2. The function f whose graph is shown in question 1 has a
removable discontinuity at which of the following points?

(A) $x = -3$ (B) $x = -1$ (C) $x = 1$
(D) $x = 3$ (E) $x = 0$

2. _____

3. Sketch a possible graph for a function f that has the stated

   properties. $f(-2)$ exists, $\lim\limits_{x \to -2} f(x)$ exists,

   f is not continuous at $x = -2$, and $\lim\limits_{x \to 1} f(x)$ does not exist.

3.
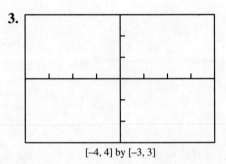

[–4, 4] by [–3, 3]

4. Find the average rate of change of the function $f(x) = 2x^2$
over the interval $[1, 3]$.

(A) 4   (B) 8   (C) 12   (D) 15   (E) 16

4. _____

5. Find the slope of the curve $y = x^2 + x$ at $x = 3$.

(A) 7   (B) 8   (C) 9   (D) 10   (E) 11

5. _____

6. Let $f(x) = \begin{cases} x^2 - 2, & x \le 1 \\ 1.5x - 2.5, & x > 1 \end{cases}$

6. _____

   Determine whether the curve $y = f(x)$ has a tangent at
   $x = 1$. If it does, give its slope.

(A) 1.5   (B) 2   (C) 2.5
(D) 3   (E) No tangent

7. The equation for free fall on Mars is $s = 6.1t^2$ ft,
where t is in seconds. Assume a rock is dropped from
a 50-ft cliff. Find the speed of the rock at $t = 1.5$ sec.

(A) 3 ft/sec   (B) 9.15 ft/sec
(C) 13.725 ft/sec   (D) 18.3 ft/sec
(E) 23.2 ft/sec

7. _____

Directions: Show all steps leading to your answers, including any intermediate results obtained using a graphing utility. Use the back of the test or another sheet of paper if necessary.

1. Use the graph to estimate the limits and value of the function, or explain why the limits do not exist.

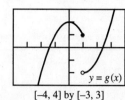

[−4, 4] by [−3, 3]

(a) $\lim\limits_{x \to 1^-} g(x)$

(b) $\lim\limits_{x \to 1^+} g(x)$

(c) $\lim\limits_{x \to 1} g(x)$

(d) $g(1)$

1. (a) _____

(b) _____

(c) _____

(d) _____

2. Determine the limit by substitution.

$$\lim\limits_{x \to -2} (5x^2 + 4x - 2)$$

2. _____

3. Assume that $\lim\limits_{x \to b} f(x) = 5$ and $\lim\limits_{x \to b} g(x) = -2$. Find the value of $\lim\limits_{x \to b} (f(x) - g(x))$.

(A) −10   (B) −7   (C) −3   (D) 3   (E) 7

3. _____

4. Find the limit graphically. Show how the Sandwich Theorem can be used to confirm your answer.

$$\lim\limits_{x \to 0} \left(3 + x^2 \sin \frac{1}{x}\right)$$

4. _____

_____

_____

5. For $f(x) = \dfrac{2x + 5}{|3x - 4|}$, use graphs and tables to find

(a) $\lim\limits_{x \to \infty} f(x)$ and (b) $\lim\limits_{x \to -\infty} f(x)$.

(c) Identify any horizontal asymptotes.

5. (a) _____

(b) _____

(c) _____

6. Consider the function $f(x)$ given to the right. Which of the following appear to be true about $f(x)$?

I. The line $y = \dfrac{1}{2}$ is a horizontal asymptote.

II. $\lim\limits_{x \to 2} f(x) = 2$

III. The line $x = 1$ is a vertical asymptote.

IV. $\lim\limits_{x \to +\infty} f(x) = \lim\limits_{x \to -\infty} f(x)$

6. _____

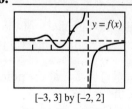

[−3, 3] by [−2, 2]

(A) I and III

(B) I, II, and III

(C) I, III, and IV

(D) I, II, III, and IV

(E) III and IV

7. **(a)** Find the vertical asymptotes of the graph of

$$f(x) = \frac{3-x}{x^2-16}$$

   (b) Describe the behavior of $f(x)$ to the left and right of each vertical asymptote.

7. **(a)** _____

   (b) _____

   _____

   _____

8. For the function $y = e^x - 2x^3 + 15x$, find:
   (a) a simple basic function right end behavior model, and
   (b) a simple basic function left end behavior model.

8. **(a)** _____

   (b) _____

9. Find the points of discontinuity of the function
   $y = \frac{x^2 + x - 2}{x^2 + 5x + 6}$. For each discontinuity, identify
   the type of discontinuity (removable, jump, infinite, or oscillating).

9. _____

   _____

10. Find a value a so that the function

$$f(x) = \begin{cases} 2x - 5, & x < 2 \\ ax^2, & x \geq 2 \end{cases} \text{ is continuous.}$$

10. _____

11. Sketch a possible graph for a function f, where $f(-2)$ exists, $\lim\limits_{x \to -2} f(x) = 2$, and f is not continuous at $x = -2$.

11.

[–4, 4] by [–3, 3]

12. Use the concept of composite functions to explain why $h(x) = |x^2 - 4x - 6|$ is a continuous function.

12. _____

   _____

   _____

13. Find the average rate of change of the function $f(x) = x^3 - 2x + 4$ over the interval $[-3, 5]$.

13. _____

14. For the function $f(x) = 5x^2$ at the point $(2, 20)$, find
    (a) the slope of the curve
    (b) an equation of the tangent line
    (c) an equation of the normal line

14. **(a)** _____

    (b) _____

    (c) _____

15. The equation for free fall at the surface of the planet Quixon is $s = 3.8t^2$ m with t in sec. Assume a rock is dropped from the top of a 400-m cliff. Find the speed of the rock at $t = 6$ sec.

15. _____

Directions: Show all steps leading to your answers, including any intermediate results obtained using a graphing utility. Use the back of the test or another sheet of paper if necessary.

1. Use the graph to estimate the limits and value of the function, or explain why the limits do not exist.

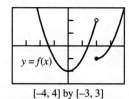

$y = f(x)$

[–4, 4] by [–3, 3]

   (a) $\lim\limits_{x\to 2^-} f(x)$
   (b) $\lim\limits_{x\to 2^+} f(x)$
   (c) $\lim\limits_{x\to 2} f(x)$
   (d) $f(2)$

1. (a) _____
   (b) _____
   (c) _____
   (d) _____

2. Determine the limit by substitution.

$$\lim_{x\to -3} (-6x^2 + 5x + 12)$$

2. _____

3. Assume that $\lim\limits_{x\to b} f(x) = -4$ and $\lim\limits_{x\to b} g(x) = 3$. Find the value of $\lim\limits_{x\to b} (f(x) \cdot g(x))$.

(A) -12 (B) -7 (C) 1 (D) 7 (E) 12

3. _____

4. Find the limit graphically. Show how the Sandwich Theorem can be used to confirm your answer.

$$\lim_{x\to 0} \left(5 - x^2 \cos \frac{1}{x}\right)$$

4. _____
_____
_____

5. For $f(x) = \dfrac{|5x + 2|}{-4x + 7}$, use graphs and tables to find
(a) $\lim\limits_{x\to\infty} f(x)$ and **(b)** $\lim\limits_{x\to-\infty} f(x)$.
(c) Identify any horizontal asymptotes.

5. (a) _____
   (b) _____
   (c) _____

6. Consider the function $g(x)$ given to the right. Which of the following appear to be true about $g(x)$?

  I. The line $x = \dfrac{1}{2}$ is a vertical asymptote.

  II. $\lim\limits_{x\to-1} g(x) = \dfrac{1}{2}$
  III. The line $y = -1$ is a horizontal asymptote.

  IV. $\lim\limits_{x\to+\infty} g(x) = \lim\limits_{x\to-\infty} g(x)$

(A) I and II   (B) I and III
(C) II and III   (D) II and IV
(E) II, III and IV

6. _____

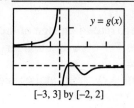

$y = g(x)$

[–3, 3] by [–2, 2]

7. **(a)** Find the vertical asymptotes of the graph of

$$f(x) = \frac{x - 1}{x^2 + 2x - 8}$$

(b) Describe the behavior of $f(x)$ to the left and right of each vertical asymptote.

7. **(a)** _____

(b) _____

_____

_____

8. For the function $y = 3x^2 - 5x + 7^{-x}$, find:
(a) a simple basic function right end behavior model, and
(b) a simple basic function left end behavior model.

8. **(a)** _____
(b) _____

9. Find the points of discontinuity of the function $y = \frac{x^2 - x - 12}{x^2 - 9}$. For each discontinuity, identify the type of discontinuity (removable, jump, infinite, or oscillating).

9. _____

_____

10. Find a value m so that the function

$$g(x) = \begin{cases} mx + 4, & x \le -3 \\ x^2 - 11, & x > -3 \end{cases} \text{ is continuous.}$$

10. _____

11. Sketch a possible graph for a function f, where $\lim_{x \to 3} f(x)$ exists, $f(3) = 1$, and f is not continuous at $x = 3$.

11.

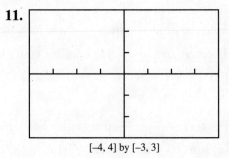

[−4, 4] by [−3, 3]

12. Use the concept of composite functions to explain why $h(x) = \sin(x^5 + 2x - 3)$ is a continuous function.

12. _____

_____

_____

13. Find the average rate of change of the function $f(x) = -2x^2 + 5x - 3$ over the interval $[-2, 7]$.

13. _____

14. For the function $f(x) = 3x^2$ at the point $(4, 48)$, find
(a) the slope of the curve
(b) an equation of the tangent line
(c) an equation of the normal line

14. **(a)** _____
(b) _____
(c) _____

15. The equation for free fall at the surface of the moon is $s = 31.8t^2$ in. with t in sec. Assume a rock is dropped from the top of a 12,000-in. cliff. Find the speed of the rock at $t = 4$ sec.

15. _____

1. Which of the following expressions does *not* give the value of $f'(3)$ for a differentiable function f?

(A) $\lim\limits_{h \to 0^+} \dfrac{f(3 + h) - f(3)}{h}$ (B) $\lim\limits_{x \to 3} \dfrac{f(x) - f(3)}{x - 3}$

(C) $\lim\limits_{h \to 0} \dfrac{f(3 + h) - f(3)}{h}$ (D) $\lim\limits_{x \to 3} \dfrac{f(x) - f(3)}{x}$

(E) $\lim\limits_{h \to 0} \dfrac{f(3 + h) - f(3 - h)}{2h}$

1. _____

2. The table below gives a driver's distance x from home along a straight road after t hours. Sketch an approximate graph of the derivative, $\dfrac{dx}{dt}$. Label your graph with the correct window dimensions.

Time t (hours)	0	1	2	3	4	5	6
Distance x (miles)	0	25	55	100	140	190	220

2.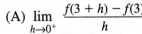

3. The graph of $y = f(x)$ is shown. At what values of x in $[-6, 6]$ does $f(x)$ appear to be nondifferentiable?

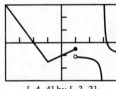

[−4, 4] by [−3, 3]

(A) $x = 1$ (B) $x = -1, x = 1$
(C) $x = -1, x = 3$ (D) $x = 1, x = 3$
(E) $x = -1, x = 1, x = 3$

3. _____

4. Which of the following describes the behavior of $y = \sqrt[4]{|x - 2|}$ at $x = 2$?

(A) differentiable   (B) corner
(C) cusp   (D) vertical tangent
(E) discontinuity

4. _____

5. Find $\dfrac{dy}{dx}$ if $y = 6x^2 - 3x + 2$.

(A) $6x - 3$ (B) $12x + 3$ (C) $12x - 3$
(D) $12x - 1$ (E) $12x^2 - 3x$

5. _____

6. Find $\dfrac{dy}{dx}$ if $y = \dfrac{2x + 5}{3x - 1}$.

(A) $\dfrac{17}{(3x - 1)^2}$ (B) $-\dfrac{17}{(3x - 1)^2}$ (C) $\dfrac{17}{(2x + 5)^2}$

(D) $\dfrac{12x + 13}{(3x - 1)^2}$ (E) $\dfrac{2}{3}$

6. _____

1. The figure shows the velocity $v = \dfrac{ds}{dt} = f(t)$, in meters per second, of a body moving along a coordinate line. Sketch a graph of the acceleration, where defined.

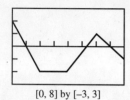

[0, 8] by [−3, 3]

1.

[0, 8] by [−3, 3]

2. In which of the following time intervals is the body moving at a constant speed?

(A) [0, 2)   (B) (2, 4)   (C) (4, 6)
(D) (6, 8]   (E) All of these

2. _____

3. Suppose the dollar cost of producing x cassettes is $c(x) = 2x + \dfrac{50}{x}$ for $x \geq 1$. Find the marginal cost when 10 cassettes are produced.

(A) $1.50   (B) $1.75   (C) $2.00
(D) $2.50   (E) $25.00

3. _____

4. Find $\dfrac{dy}{dx}$ if $y = \tan x + \sin x$

(A) $\sec^2 x + \cos x$ (B) $\sec^2 x - \cos x$

(C) $\sec x \tan x + \cos x$ (D) $\cot x + \cos x$

(E) $\sec x \tan x - \cos x$

4. _____

5. Find an approximate equation of the line tangent to the graph of $y = x \csc x$ at $x = \dfrac{\pi}{6}$.

(A) $y = 1.50x - 0.18$ (B) $y = 0.19x + 1.05$
(C) $y = 5.37x - 1.77$ (D) $y = 0.19x + 0.95$
(E) $y = 3.81x - 0.95$

5. _____

6. Find $\dfrac{dy}{dx}$ if $y = (2x + 5)^8$.

(A) $2(2x + 5)^8$ (B) $8(2x + 5)^7$ (C) $8(2x + 5)^8$
(D) $8x^7(2x + 5)$ (E) $16(2x + 5)^7$

6. _____

7. A curve is defined parametrically by $x = \cos t$ and $y = 3t + 5$. Find $\dfrac{dy}{dx}$ at the point defined by $t = \dfrac{\pi}{6}$.

(A) -6 (B) $-\dfrac{1}{2}$ (C) $-\dfrac{1}{6}$ (D) $2\sqrt{3}$ (E) 6

7. _____

1. Find $\dfrac{dy}{dx}$ if $3\cos x + \sin y = x^2$.

    1. _____

(A) $\dfrac{2x + 3\sin x}{\sin y}$ (B) $\dfrac{2x + 3\sin x}{\cos y}$ (C) $\dfrac{x^2 - 3\cos x}{\sin y}$

(D) $\dfrac{3\sin x}{\cos y}$ (E) $\dfrac{2x - 3\sin y}{\cos y}$

2. Find an equation of the line that is normal to the graph of $4x + 2x^2 y - y^2 = 23$ at $(2, 3)$.

    2. _____

(A) $y = -14x + 31$ (B) $y = 14x - 25$

(C) $y = \dfrac{1}{7}x + \dfrac{19}{7}$ (D) $y = \dfrac{1}{14}x + \dfrac{20}{7}$

(E) $y = -\dfrac{1}{14}x + \dfrac{22}{7}$

3. Which of the following *cannot* be true if $f'(x) = 7x^{4/7}$?

    3. _____

(A) $f(x) = \dfrac{49}{11}x^{11/7} + \dfrac{15}{11}$ (B) $f''(x) = 4x^{-3/7}$

(C) $f''(x) = \dfrac{4}{\sqrt[7]{x^3}}$ (D) $f'''(x) = -\dfrac{12}{7x^{10/7}}$

(E) $f'''(x) = \dfrac{12}{7}x^{-10/7}$

4. Find $\dfrac{dy}{dx}$ if $y = \sec^{-1}\sqrt{x}$.

    4. _____

(A) $\dfrac{1}{2x\sqrt{x-1}}$ (B) $\dfrac{1}{\sqrt{x^2 - x}}$ (C) $\dfrac{1}{2x\sqrt{x^2 - 1}}$

(D) $\dfrac{1}{2\sqrt{x}(1 + x)}$ (E) $\dfrac{1}{2\sqrt{x^2 - 1}}$

5. Which expression is equivalent to $\cot^{-1} x$?

    5. _____

(A) $\tan^{-1}\left(\dfrac{1}{x}\right)$ (B) $\dfrac{\cos^{-1} x}{\sin^{-1} x}$ (C) $\dfrac{1}{\cot x}$

(D) $\dfrac{\pi}{2} - \tan^{-1} x$ (E) $\tan^{-1}\left(\dfrac{\pi}{2} - x\right)$

6. Find $\dfrac{dy}{dx}$ if $y = x^3 e^{2x}$.

    6. _____

(A) $6x^2 e^{2x}$ (B) $x^3 e^{2x} + 3x^2 e^{2x}$
(C) $2x^3 e^{2x} + 3x^2 e^{2x}$ (D) $x^3 e^2 + 3x^2 e^{2x}$
(E) $x^3 e^{2x} + 6x^2 e^{2x}$

7. Find $\dfrac{dy}{dx}$ if $y = \ln(x^2 + 5x)$.

    7. _____

(A) $\dfrac{2x + 5}{\ln(x^2 + 5x)}$ (B) $\dfrac{2x + 5}{x}$ (C) $\dfrac{1}{2x + 5}$

(D) $\dfrac{2x + 5}{x^2 + 5x}$ (E) $(2x + 5)\ln(x^2 + 5x)$

               Calculus Assessment   **15**

Directions: Show all steps leading to your answers, including any intermediate results obtained using a graphing utility. Use the back of the test or another sheet of paper if necessary.

1. Use the definition of the derivative to find the derivative of $f(x) = x^2 - 3$ at $x = 2$. Show your work.

1. _____

2. Sketch a possible graph of a continuous function f that has domain $[-3, 3]$, where $f(-1) = 1$ and the graph of $y = f'(x)$ is shown below.

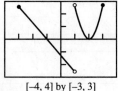

[−4, 4] by [−3, 3]

2.
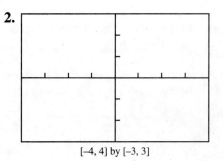
[−4, 4] by [−3, 3]

3. Which of the following describes the behavior of $y = \sqrt[3]{x + 2}$ at $x = -2$?

3. _____

(A) differentiable   (B) corner

(C) cusp   (D) vertical tangent

(E) discontinuity

4. Let $f(x) = \text{int } x$.
(a) Find NDER $(f(x), 3)$.
(b) Is your answer to part (a) a meaningful estimate of a derivative of $f(x)$? Explain.

4. (a) _____

(b) _____

_____

5. Find (a) $\dfrac{dy}{dx}$ and (b) $\dfrac{d^2y}{dx^2}$ if $y = 3x^4 - 9x^3 + 5x$.

5. (a) _____

(b) _____

6. Suppose that u and v are differentiable at $x = 5$ and that $u(5) = 7$, $v(5) = 2$, $u'(5) = -3$, and $v'(5) = 6$. Find (a) $\dfrac{d}{dx}\left(\dfrac{u}{v}\right)$ and (b) $\dfrac{d}{dx}(10uv)$ at $x = 5$.

6. (a) _____

(b) _____

7. A particle moves along a line so that its position at any time $t \geq 0$ is given by the function $s(t) = t^3 - 8t + 1$, where s is measured in feet and t is measured in seconds.
(a) Find the displacement during the first 3 seconds.
(b) Find the average velocity during the first 3 seconds.
(c) Find the instantaneous velocity when $t = 3$.
(d) Find the acceleration of the particle when $t = 3$.
(e) At what value or values of t does the particle change direction?

7. (a) _____
(b) _____
(c) _____
(d) _____
(e) _____

---

8. The coordinates *s* of a moving body for various values of *t* are given.

t (sec)	0	0.5	1.0	1.5	2.0	2.5	3.0	3.5	4.0
s (ft)	−19.5	−6	4.5	12	16.5	18	16.5	12	4.5

8. (a)

[0, 4] by [−20, 20]

(a) Plot *s* versus *t*, and sketch a smooth curve through the given points.

(b) Assuming this smooth curve represents the motion of the body, estimate the velocity at $t = 1.0$, $t = 2.5$, and $t = 3.5$.

(b) $t = 1.0$: _____

$t = 2.5$: _____

$t = 3.5$: _____

9. Find $\dfrac{dy}{dx}$ if $y = \dfrac{\cos x}{1 + \tan x}$.

9. _____

10. Find the points on the graph of $y = \sec x$, $0 \le x \le 2\pi$, where the tangent is parallel to the line $3y - 2x = 4$.

10. _____

11. Find $\dfrac{dy}{dx}$ for $y = \sin(x^2 - 1)$.

11. _____

12. A curve is parametrized by the equations $x = \sqrt{t}$ and $y = (t - 3)^2$. Find an equation of the line tangent to the curve at the point defined by $t = 9$.

12. _____

13. Which of the following could be true if $f''(t) = t^{-2/3}$?

I. $f(t) = \dfrac{9}{4}t^{4/3}$

II. $f'(t) = 7 - 3t^{1/3}$

III. $f'''(t) = -\dfrac{2}{3}t^{-5/3}$

(A) I and II   (B) I and III   (C) I only
(D) III only   (E) I, II, and III

13. _____

14. Use implicit differentiation to find $\dfrac{dy}{dx}$ if $x^2 + 5xy + y^5 = 8$.

14. _____

15. Find $\dfrac{dy}{dx}$ if $y = \tan^{-1}\left(\dfrac{1}{2x}\right)$.

15. _____

16. Find $\dfrac{dy}{dx}$ if $y = 4^{-x+3}$.

16. _____

17. Which of the following expressions has the same derivative as $y = \log x$?

(A) $\log_6 x$ (B) $\log 5x$ (C) $\log x^2$

(D) $3 \log x$ (E) $\log \dfrac{1}{x}$

17. _____

Directions: Show all steps leading to your answers, including any intermediate results obtained using a graphing utility. Use the back of the test or another sheet of paper if necessary.

1. Use the definition of the derivative to find the derivative of $f(x) = x^2 + x$ at $x = 5$. Show your work.

1. _____

2. Sketch a possible graph of a continuous function f that has domain $[-3, 3]$, where $f(-1) = -1$ and the graph of $y = f'(x)$ is shown below.

2.
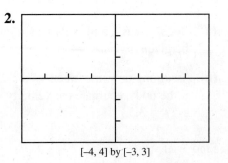
[–4, 4] by [–3, 3]

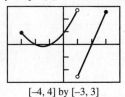
[–4, 4] by [–3, 3]

3. Which of the following describes the behavior of

$y = \left| x^2 - 16 \right|$ at $x = 4$?

3. _____

   (A) differentiable   (B) corner

   (C) cusp   (D) vertical tangent

   (E) discontinuity

4. Let $f(x) = \sqrt[3]{x - 2}$.
   (a) Find NDER $(f(x), 2)$.
   (b) Is your answer to part (a) a meaningful estimate of a derivative of $f(x)$? Explain.

4. (a) _____
    (b) _____
        _____

5. Find **(a)** $\dfrac{dy}{dx}$ and **(b)** $\dfrac{d^2y}{dx^2}$ if $y = 7x^3 + 4x^2 - 6x$.

5. (a) _____

    (b) _____

6. Suppose that u and v are differentiable at $x = 2$ and that

$u(2) = 4$, $v(2) = -9$, $u'(2) = 5$, and $v'(2) = 3$.

Find **(a)** $\dfrac{d}{dx}(6uv)$ and **(b)** $\dfrac{d}{dx}\left(\dfrac{u}{v}\right)$ at $x = 2$.

6. (a) _____

    (b) _____

7. A particle moves along a line so that its position at any time $t \geq 0$ is given by the function $s(t) = 2t^3 - 5t - 3$, where s is measured in feet and t is measured in seconds.
   (a) Find the displacement during the first 5 seconds.
   (b) Find the average velocity during the first 5 seconds.
   (c) Find the instantaneous velocity when $t = 5$.
   (d) Find the acceleration of the particle when $t = 5$.
   (e) At what value or values of t does the particle change direction?

7. (a) _____
    (b) _____
    (c) _____
    (d) _____
    (e) _____

8. The coordinates s of a moving body for various values of t are given.

8. (a)

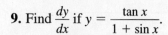

t (sec)	0	0.5	1.0	1.5	2.0	2.5	3.0	3.5	4.0
s (ft)	-12	-15	-16	-15	-12	-7	0	9	20

(a) Plot s versus t, and sketch a smooth curve through the given points.

[0, 4] by [–20, 20]

(b) Assuming this smooth curve represents the motion of the body, estimate the velocity at $t = 1.0$, $t = 2.5$, and $t = 3.5$.

(b) $t = 1.0$: _____

      $t = 2.5$: _____

      $t = 3.5$: _____

9. Find $\dfrac{dy}{dx}$ if $y = \dfrac{\tan x}{1 + \sin x}$.

9. _____

10. Find the points on the graph of $y = \tan x$, $0 \le x \le 2\pi$, where the tangent is parallel to the line $4x - y = 7$.

10. _____

11. Find $\dfrac{dy}{dx}$ for $y = \cos 5x^3$.

11. _____

12. A curve is parametrized by the equations $x = t^2 - 6t$ and $y = 8\sqrt{t - 2}$. Find an equation of the line tangent to the curve at the point defined by $t = 6$.

12. _____

13. Which of the following could be true if $f''(t) = \dfrac{1}{4}t^{-3/4}$?

    I. $f(t) = \dfrac{4}{5}t^{5/4} + 6t$

    II. $f'(t) = t^{1/4}$

    III. $f'''(t) = -\dfrac{3}{16}t^{-7/4}$

    (A) I and II   (B) II and III   (C) I only

    (D) III only   (E) I, II, and III

13. _____

14. Use implicit differentiation to find $\dfrac{dy}{dx}$ if $x^3 + 4xy^2 - y^4 = 7$.

14. _____

15. Find $\dfrac{dy}{dx}$ if $y = \sin^{-1}(3x)$.

15. _____

16. Find $\dfrac{dy}{dx}$ if $y = 3^{2x+5}$.

16. _____

17. Which of the following expressions does *not* have the same derivative as $y = \log_3 x$?

    (A) $16 + \log_3 x$ (B) $\log_3 4x$ (C) $\dfrac{1}{2}\log_6 x$

    (D) $\dfrac{\ln x}{\ln 3}$ (E) $\log_9 x^2$, $x > 0$

17. _____

1. Find the (absolute) extreme values of the function whose graph is shown.

1. _____

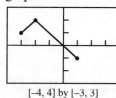

[−4, 4] by [−3, 3]

(A) Minimum −3, maximum 1
(B) Minimum −3, maximum 2
(C) Minimum −1, maximum 1
(D) Minimum −1, maximum 2
(E) Minimum 1, maximum −2

2. Find the values of x where the extreme values of the function $y = 2x^3 − 9x^2 − 24x$ occur.

2. _____

(A) $x = −4, x = 1$ (B) $x = −1, x = 4$
(C) $x = 1, x = 4$ (D) $x = −112, x = 13$
(E) $x \approx −1.88, x = 0, x \approx 6.38$

3. Find the (absolute) minimum value of the function $f(x) = \frac{1}{4}x^4 + x^3 − 5x^2$.

3. _____

(A) −93.75   (B) 35   (C) −35
(D) −8   (E) 0

4. Find the interval or intervals on which the function whose graph is shown is increasing.

4. _____

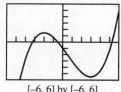

[−6, 6] by [−6, 6]

(A) $(−\infty, −0.5]$
(B) $[0.5, \infty)$
(C) $[−3.5, 3.5]$
(D) $[−2, 3]$
(E) $(−\infty, −2] \cup [3, \infty)$

5. The graph of $y = \cos x$ is concave down on which of the following intervals?

5. _____

(A) $(−\pi, 0)$ (B) $(0, \pi)$ (C) $(0, 2\pi)$
(D) $\left(−\dfrac{\pi}{2}, \dfrac{\pi}{2}\right)$ (E) $\left(\dfrac{\pi}{2}, \dfrac{3\pi}{2}\right)$

6. Find the function whose derivative is $f'(x) = 6x − 8$ and whose graph passes through the point $P(2, 6)$.

6. _____

(A) $f(x) = 6$ (B) $f(x) = 6x − 6$
(C) $f(x) = 3x^2 − 8x$ (D) $f(x) = 3x^2 − 8x + 10$
(E) $f(x) = 6x^2 − 8x − 2$

7. Let $y = f(x)$ be continuous on the closed interval $[a, b]$ and differentiable on the open interval (a, b). Then, according to the Mean Value Theorem, there is at least one point c in (a, b) at which

7. _____

(A) $f(c) = \dfrac{f'(b) − f'(a)}{b − a}$ (B) $f'(c) = \dfrac{f(b) − f(a)}{b − a}$

(C) $f'(c) = \dfrac{f'(b) − f'(a)}{b − a}$ (D) $f(c) = \dfrac{f(a) + f(b)}{b − a}$

(E) $f'(c) = \dfrac{f'(a) + f'(b)}{b − a}$

1. You are designing a rectangular poster to contain 256 in^2 of printing with a 3-in. margin at the top and bottom and a 2-in. margin at each side. What overall dimensions will minimize the amount of paper used? (Round to the nearest whole inch if necessary.)

   (A) 13 in. by 20 in.   (B) 15 in. by 23 in.
   (C) 17 in. by 26 in.   (D) 19 in. by 23 in.
   (E) 20 in. by 22 in.

1. _____

2. A rectangle with its base on the x-axis is to be inscribed under the graph of $y = 2 - x^2$. Find the height of the rectangle if the area is the largest possible area. (Round to the nearest hundredth.)

   (A) 0.82   (B) 1.33   (C) 2.18   (D) 1.64   (E) 0.67

2. _____

3. Use the linear approximation $(1 + x)^k \approx 1 + kx$ to find an approximation for the function $f(x) = \dfrac{1}{\sqrt{4 + x}}$ for values of x near zero.

   (A) $\dfrac{1}{2} - \dfrac{x}{8}$ (B) $\dfrac{1}{2} - \dfrac{x}{16}$ (C) $\dfrac{1}{2} - \dfrac{x}{32}$

   (D) $\dfrac{1}{4} - \dfrac{x}{8}$ (E) $\dfrac{1}{4} - \dfrac{x}{32}$

3. _____

4. You are using Newton's method to solve $x^3 - 5x - 2 = 0$. If your first guess is $x_1 = 2$, what value will you calculate for the next approximation x_2? (Round to the nearest hundredth.)

   (A) 1.43   (B) 2.41   (C) 2.43   (D) 2.51   (E) 2.57

4. _____

5. Let $y = \sin(x^2 - 3)$. Find dy.

   (A) $dy = 2x \sin (x^2 - 3) \, dx$ (B) $dy = 2x \cos (x^2 - 3)$
   (C) $dy = 2x \cos (x^2 - 3) \, dx$ (D) $dy = -2x \cos (x^2 - 3) \, dx$
   (E) $dy = \cos (x^2 - 3) \, dx$

5. _____

6. The volume of a right circular cone is given by

   $V = \dfrac{1}{3}\pi r^2 h$, where r is the radius and h is the height.
   Find $\dfrac{dV}{dt}$ if $r = 4$, $h = 5$, $\dfrac{dr}{dt} = 6$, and $\dfrac{dh}{dt} = -3$.

   (A) -16π (B) 4π (C) 32π (D) 64π (E) 80π

6. _____

7. A woman 5.5 ft tall walks at a rate of 6 ft/sec toward a streetlight that is 22 ft above the ground. At what rate is the length of her shadow changing when she is 15 ft from the base of the light? (Round to the nearest 0.5 ft/sec if necessary.)

   (A) -2.0 ft/sec   (B) -1.5 ft/sec   (C) 1.5 ft/sec
   (D) 2.0 ft/sec   (E) 2.5 ft/sec

7. _____

Directions: Show all steps leading to your answers, including any intermediate results obtained using a graphing utility. Use the back of the test or another sheet of paper if necessary.

1. Use the graph of $y = f(x)$ to estimate the answer to the following questions.
   (a) Find the local extreme values and where they occur.
   (b) For what values of x is $f'(x) > 0$?
   (c) For what values of x is $f'(x) < 0$?
   (d) For what values of x is $f''(x) > 0$?
   (e) For what values of x is $f''(x) < 0$?

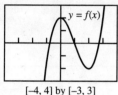

   [−4, 4] by [−3, 3]

1. (a) Min: _____ at $x = $ _____
       Max: _____ at $x = $ _____
   (b) _____
   (c) _____
   (d) _____
   (e) _____

2. For $y = x^4 - 72x^2 - 17$, use analytic methods to find the exact intervals on which the function is
   (a) increasing,   (b) decreasing,
   (c) concave up,   (d) concave down.
   Then find any
   (e) local extreme values,   (f) inflection points.

2. (a) _____
   (b) _____
   (c) _____
   (d) _____
   (e) Min: _____ at $x = $ _____
       Max: _____ at $x = $ _____
   (f) _____

3. For $y = \dfrac{3x}{2e^x + e^{-x}}$, use graphing techniques to find the approximate intervals on which the function is
   (a) increasing,   (b) decreasing,
   (c) concave up,   (d) concave down.
   Then find any
   (e) local extreme values,   (f) inflection points.

3. (a) _____
   (b) _____
   (c) _____
   (d) _____
   (e) Min: _____ at $x = $ _____
       Max: _____ at $x = $ _____
   (f) _____

4. The derivative of a function is $f'(x) = (x - 1)^2(x + 3)$. Find the value of x at each point where f has a
   (a) local maximum,   (b) local minimum, or
   (c) point of inflection.

4. (a) _____
   (b) _____
   (c) _____

5. The derivative of a function is $g'(x) = 4x + 1$ and the graph of g passes through the point $P(5, 3)$. Find $g(x)$.

5. _____

6. You are planning to make an open rectangular box from a 12- by 14-cm piece of cardboard by cutting congruent squares from the corners and folding up the sides.

   (a) What are the dimensions of the box of largest volume you can make this way?

   (b) What is its volume?

6. (a) _____
   (b) _____

7. Assume that *f* is continuous on $[-4, 4]$ and differentiable on $(-4, 4)$. The table gives some values of $f'(x)$.

x	-4	-3	-2	-1	0	1	2	3	4
$f'(x)$	74	39	10	-6	-14	-12	0	22	55

(a) Estimate where *f* is increasing, decreasing, and has local extrema.

(b) Find a quadratic regression equation for the data in the table.

(c) Use the model in (b) for f' and find a formula for *f* that satisfies $f(0) = 0$.

7. (a) Increasing: _____
Decreasing: _____
Local min: $x \approx$ _____
Local max: $x \approx$ _____
(b) _____
(c) _____

8. Let $f(x) = x^3 + ax^2$. What is the value of *a* if
(a) *f* has a local minimum at $x = 4$?
(b) *f* has a point of inflection at $x = 6$?

8. (a) _____
(b) _____

9. Suppose the revenue, in dollars, for producing *x* chairs is given by $r(x) = 50x$ and the cost to produce the chairs is given by $c(x) = 0.001x^3 - 0.1x^2 + 12x + 1500$. Find the production level that will maximize profit.

(A) 37 chairs   (B) 123 chairs   (C) 151 chairs
(D) 235 chairs   (E) Not here, or does not exist

9. _____

10. Find the linearization $L(x)$ of $f(x) = 3x - \dfrac{2}{x^2}$ at $x = 2$.

10. _____

11. Use Newton's method to estimate all real solutions of the equation $x^3 - 3x^2 + 2x - \cos x = 0$. Make your solutions accurate to 6 decimal places.

11. _____

12. Let $y = \ln(5x - 2)$.

(a) Find *dy* and **(b)** estimate *dy* for $x = 2$ and $dx = 0.03$.

12. (a) _____
(b) _____

13. The base of a pyramid-shaped tank is a square with sides of length 12 feet, and the vertex of the pyramid is 10 feet above the base. The tank is filled to a depth of 4 feet, and water is flowing into the tank at the rate of 2 cubic feet per minute. Find the rate of change of the depth of water in the tank. (Hint: The volume of a pyramid is given by $V = \dfrac{1}{3}Bh$, where *B* is the base area and *h* is the height of the pyramid.)

13. _____

14. Two cars are approaching an intersection along roads that make a 90° angle. The first car is 100 feet from the intersection and is traveling at a rate of 30 feet per second. The second car is 150 feet from the intersection and is traveling at a rate of 40 feet per second. Find the rate of change of the distance between the cars.

14. _____

Directions: Show all steps leading to your answers, including any intermediate results obtained using a graphing utility. Use the back of the test or another sheet of paper if necessary.

1. Use the graph of $y = f(x)$ to estimate the answer to the following questions.
   (a) Find the local extreme values and where they occur.
   (b) For what values of x is $f'(x) > 0$?
   (c) For what values of x is $f'(x) < 0$?
   (d) For what values of x is $f''(x) > 0$?
   (e) For what values of x is $f''(x) < 0$?

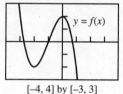

[-4, 4] by [-3, 3]

1. (a) Min: _____ at $x =$ _____
          Max: _____ at $x =$ _____
   (b) _____
   (c) _____
   (d) _____
   (e) _____

2. For $y = -x^4 + 18x^2 + 11$, use analytic methods to find the exact intervals on which the function is
   (a) increasing,   **(b)** decreasing,
   (c) concave up,   **(d)** concave down.
   Then find any
   (e) local extreme values,   **(f)** inflection points.

2. (a) _____
   (b) _____
   (c) _____
   (d) _____
   (e) Min: _____ at $x =$ _____
          Max: _____ at $x =$ _____
   (f) _____

3. For $y = \dfrac{e^x}{5x^2 + 1}$, use graphing techniques to find the approximate intervals on which the function is
   (a) increasing,   **(b)** decreasing,
   (c) concave up,   **(d)** concave down.
   Then find any
   (e) local extreme values,   **(f)** inflection points.

3. (a) _____
   (b) _____
   (c) _____
   (d) _____
   (e) Min: _____ at $x =$ _____
          Max: _____ at $x =$ _____
   (f) _____

4. The derivative of a function is $f'(x) = (x + 2)^2(x - 4)$. Find the value of x at each point where f has a
   (a) local maximum,   **(b)** local minimum, or
   (c) point of inflection.

4. (a) _____
   (b) _____
   (c) _____

5. The derivative of a function is $g'(x) = 6x^2$ and the graph of g passes through the point $P(3, 7)$. Find $g(x)$.

5. _____

6. You are planning to make an open rectangular box from a 10- by 18-cm piece of cardboard by cutting congruent squares from the corners and folding up the sides.

   (a) What are the dimensions of the box of largest volume you can make this way?

   (b) What is its volume?

6. (a) _____
   (b) _____

7. Assume that f is continuous on $[-4, 4]$ and differentiable on $(-4, 4)$. The table gives some values of $f'(x)$.

x	-4	-3	-2	-1	0	1	2	3	4
$f'(x)$	-55	-22	3	21	30	32	20	0	-40

(a) Estimate where f is increasing, decreasing, and has local extrema.

(b) Find a quadratic regression equation for the data in the table.

(c) Use the model in (b) for f' and find a formula for f that satisfies $f(0) = 0$.

7. (a) Increasing: _____
   Decreasing: _____
   Local min: $x \approx$ _____
   Local max: $x \approx$ _____

(b) _____

(c) _____

8. Let $f(x) = x^4 + ax^2$. What is the value of a if
   (a) f has a local minimum at $x = 5$?
   (b) f has a point of inflection at $x = 2$?

8. (a) _____
   (b) _____

9. Suppose the revenue, in dollars, for producing x bicycles is given by $r(x) = 90x$ and the cost to produce the bicycles is given by $c(x) = 0.0002x^3 - 0.1x^2 + 20x + 6000$. Find the production level that will maximize profit.

   (A) 28 bicycles   (B) 547 bicycles   (C) 586 bicycles
   (D) 883 bicycles   (E) Not here, or does not exist

9. _____

10. Find the linearization $L(x)$ of $f(x) = x^2 + \dfrac{4}{x}$ at $x = 4$.

10. _____

11. Use Newton's method to estimate all real solutions of the equation $x^3 - 2x^2 - 2 - 2\sin x = 0$. Make your solutions accurate to 6 decimal places.

11. _____

12. Let $y = e^{3x-5}$.

    (a) Find dy and (b) estimate dy for $x = 2$ and $dx = 0.04$.

12. (a) _____
    (b) _____

13. The base of a cone-shaped tank is a circle of radius 5 feet, and the vertex of the cone is 12 feet above the base. The tank is filled to a depth of 7 feet, and water is flowing out of the tank at the rate of 3 cubic feet per minute. Find the rate of change of the depth of water in the tank.

    (Hint: The volume of a cone is given by $V = \dfrac{1}{3}Bh$,

    where B is the base area and h is the height of the cone.)

13. _____

14. Two boats are traveling away from a buoy along paths that make a 90° angle. The first boat is 165 feet from the buoy and is traveling at a rate of 25 feet per second. The second boat is 110 feet from the buoy and is traveling at a rate of 35 feet per second. Find the rate of change of the distance between the boats.

14. _____

1. The table shows the velocity of a bicyclist riding for 30 seconds. Use the right-endpoint values (RRAM) to estimate the distance using 6 intervals of length 5.

1. _____

Time (sec)	0	5	10	15	20	25	30
Velocity (ft/sec)	0	6	12	18	26	24	22

(A) 107 ft   (B) 430 ft   (C) 485 ft
(D) 525 ft   (E) 540 ft

2. Sketch the region R enclosed between the graph of $y = -\frac{1}{2}x^2 + 3x - \frac{5}{2}$ and the x-axis for $1 \leq x \leq 5$. Partition $[1, 5]$ into 4 subintervals and show the four rectangles that MRAM uses to approximate the area of R.

2.

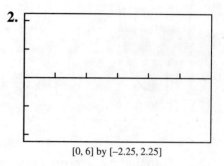

[0, 6] by [–2.25, 2.25]

3. Find MRAM_4 for the region described in question 2.

3. _____

(A) 4.625   (B) 5.125   (C) 5.0   (D) 5.5   (E) 6.0

4. Which definite integral can be expressed as
$$\lim_{\|P\|\to 0} \sum_{k=1}^{n} \left(3c_k^2 + 2c_k\right)\Delta x,$$ where P is any partition of $[3, 7]$?

4. _____

(A) $\int_3^7 (3x^2 + 2)x \, dx$ (B) $\int_3^7 (3x^2 + 2x) \, dx$

(C) $\int_3^7 (6x + 2)dx$ (D) $\int_3^7 (x^3 + x^2) \, dx$

(E) $\int_7^3 (3x^2 + 2x) \, dx$

5. Use the graph of the integrand and areas to evaluate $\int_0^5 \sqrt{25 - x^2}dx.$

5. _____

(A) $\frac{25}{2}$ (B) $\frac{5\pi}{2}$ (C) $\frac{25\pi}{4}$ (D) $\frac{25\pi}{2}$ (E) 25π

6. Suppose that $\int_5^7 f(x) \, dx = 6$ and $\int_5^7 g(x) \, dx = 10$. Which of the following is *not* necessarily true?

6. _____

(A) $\int_5^7 5g(x) \, dx = 50$ (B) $\int_5^7 [f(x) + g(x)] \, dx = 16$

(C) $\int_5^7 [f(x)g(x)] \, dx = 60$ (D) $\int_5^7 [f(x) - g(x)] \, dx = -4$

(E) $\int_5^7 [2f(x) - 3g(x)] \, dx = -18$

7. Find the average value of the function $y = 3x^2 - 2x$ on the interval $[2, 4]$.

7. _____

(A) 22   (B) 30   (C) 34   (D) 48   (E) 52

1. Evaluate $\int_{1}^{6} \dfrac{4}{x^3}\,dx$ using Part 2 of the Fundamental Theorem.

    1.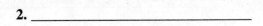

  (A) $-\dfrac{35}{18}$ (B) $\dfrac{35}{18}$ (C) $-\dfrac{35}{36}$ (D) $\dfrac{35}{36}$ (E) $\dfrac{1295}{108}$

2. Find the area of the shaded region.

    2. _____

  (A) $\dfrac{8\pi}{3}$

  (B) $\dfrac{8\pi}{3} + \dfrac{2}{\sqrt{3}}$

  (C) $\dfrac{8\pi}{3} - 2\sqrt{3}$

  (D) $\dfrac{8\pi}{3} + 2\sqrt{3}$

  (E) $2\sqrt{3}$

$y = \csc^2 x$

3. Use NINT to find the approximate value of $\int_{2.6}^{3.8} \dfrac{\sin^2 x}{4 - x}\,dx.$

    3. _____

  (A) -1.78 (B) 0.30 (C) 1.18 (D) 1.64 (E) 1.78

4. Find $\dfrac{dy}{dx}$ if $y = \int_{0}^{2x} (t^2 + 5t - 3)\,dt.$

    4. _____

  (A) $2x + 5$ (B) $x^2 + 5x - 3$

  (C) $2x^2 + 10x - 3$ (D) $8x^2 + 20x - 6$

  (E) $4x^2 + 10x - 3$

5. Use the Trapezoidal Rule with $n = 3$ to approximate the value of $\int_{2}^{8} 2x^3\,dx.$

    5. _____

  (A) 1152 (B) 1980 (C) 2070

  (D) 2160 (E) 3168

6. Use Simpson's Rule with $n = 4$ to approximate the value of $\int_{-2}^{2} (3x - 5)^3\,dx.$

    6. _____

  (A) -1830 (B) -1310 (C) -1220

  (D) -1175 (E) -957

7. Which of the following methods will typically give the most accurate approximation of the value of a definite integral? (Assume the same number of intervals are used for each method.)

    7. _____

  (A) Trapezoidal Rule   (B) Left-endpoint rectangles

  (C) Midpoint rectangles   (D) Simpson's Rule

  (E) Right-endpoint rectangles

Directions: Show all steps leading to your answers, including any intermediate results obtained using a graphing utility. Use the back of the test or another sheet of paper if necessary.

1. Consider the region enclosed between the graph of $f(x) = x^2 - \ln x$ and the x-axis for $1 \le x \le 5$.
   (a) Find MRAM_4, the area estimate obtained using 4 midpoint rectangles.
   (b) Use MRAM to estimate the area with accuracy of 2 decimal places.

1. (a) _____
    (b) _____

2. A solid is formed by revolving the curve $y = x^{2/3} + 1$, $0 \le x \le 2.5$, about the x-axis. Estimate the volume of the solid by partitioning $[0, 2.5]$ into five subintervals of equal length, slicing the solid with planes perpendicular to the x-axis at the subintervals' left endpoints, and constructing cylinders of height 0.5 based on cross sections at these points, as shown at the right.

2. _____

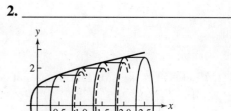

3. Use an area to evaluate $\displaystyle\int_a^{a^2} 3x\, dx$, where $a > 1$.

3. _____

4. Use NINT to evaluate $\displaystyle\int_3^{7.2} \frac{e^x - \sin x}{x}\, dx$.

4. _____

5. Suppose that f and g are continuous functions and that $\displaystyle\int_3^5 f(x)\, dx = 7$, $\displaystyle\int_3^5 g(x)\, dx = 2$, and $\displaystyle\int_0^5 g(x)\, dx = 4$. Which of the following must be true?

5. _____

  I. $\displaystyle\int_0^3 g(x)\, dx = 2$

  II. $\displaystyle\int_3^5 [f(x)g(x)]\, dx = 14$

  III. $\displaystyle\int_3^5 [f(x) - g(x)]\, dx = 5$

  (A) I and II   (B) I and III   (C) II and III
  (D) III only   (E) I, II, and III

6. Evaluate $\displaystyle\int_2^7 (4x - 10)\, dx$.

6. _____

7. Evaluate $\displaystyle\int_0^{\pi/3} \sec x \tan x\, dx$ using Part 2 of the Fundamental Theorem of Calculus.

7. _____

8. (a) Graph the function $y = 0.2x^2 - 0.8x - 1$ over the interval $[0, 6]$.

(b) Integrate $y = 0.2x^2 - 0.8x - 1$ over $[0, 6]$.

(c) Find the area of the region between the graph in part (a) and the x-axis.

8. (a)

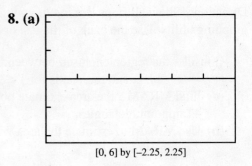

[0, 6] by [–2.25, 2.25]

(b) _____

(c) _____

9. (a) Let $f(x) = 4 - 3x$. Find K so that

$$\int_{-1}^{x} f(t)\, dt + K = \int_{3}^{x} f(t)\, dt.$$

(b) Find $\dfrac{d}{dx}\displaystyle\int_{-1}^{x} f(t)\, dt$.

9. (a) _____

(b) _____

10. A particle moves along a coordinate axis. Its position at time t (sec) is

$$s(t) = \int_{0}^{t} f(x)\, dx \text{ cm, where}$$

f is the function whose graph is shown.

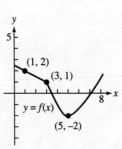

10. (a) _____

(b) _____

(c) _____

(d) _____

(e) _____

(a) What is the particle's position at $t = 0$?

(b) What is the particle's position at $t = 3$?

(c) What is the particle's velocity at $t = 5$?

(d) Approximately when is the acceleration zero?

(e) At what time during the first 7 sec does s have its largest value?

11. Use the Trapezoidal Rule with $n = 4$ to approximate the value of $\displaystyle\int_{0}^{2} (x^2 - x)\, dx$.

11. _____

12. A meadow has the shape shown, where the measurements shown were taken at 30-foot intervals. Use Simpson's Rule to estimate the area of the meadow.

12. _____

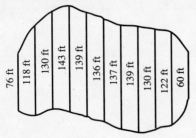

Directions: Show all steps leading to your answers, including any intermediate results obtained using a graphing utility. Use the back of the test or another sheet of paper if necessary.

1. Consider the region enclosed between the graph of $f(x) = e^x + x^3$ and the x-axis for $1 \leq x \leq 3.5$.
   (a) Find MRAM_5, the area estimate obtained using 5 midpoint rectangles.
   (b) Use MRAM to estimate the area with accuracy of 2 decimal places.

1. (a) _____
   (b) _____

2. A solid is formed by revolving the curve $y = 4 - x^{3/4}$, $0 \leq x \leq 4$, about the x-axis. Estimate the volume of the solid by partitioning $[0, 4]$ into four subintervals of equal length, slicing the solid with planes perpendicular to the x-axis at the subintervals' right endpoints, and constructing cylinders of height 1 based on cross sections at these points, as shown at the right.

2. _____

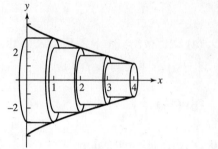

3. Use an area to evaluate $\int_{a^2}^{b} 5x \, dx$, where $b > a^2$.

3. _____

4. Use NINT to evaluate $\int_{4.1}^{8} \frac{\ln x}{x + \cos x} \, dx$.

4. _____

5. Suppose that g and h are continuous functions and that $\int_{2}^{6} g(x) \, dx = 5$, $\int_{2}^{6} h(x) \, dx = -1$, and $\int_{5}^{6} h(x) \, dx = 3$. Which of the following must be true?

5. _____

   I. $\int_{2}^{6} \frac{g(x)}{h(x)} \, dx = -5$

   II. $\int_{5}^{6} 4h(x) \, dx = 12$

   III. $\int_{2}^{5} h(x) = -4$

   (A) I and II   (B) I and III   (C) II and III
   (D) III only   (E) I, II, and III

6. Evaluate $\int_{3}^{8} (-6x + 4) \, dx$.

6. _____

7. Evaluate $\int_{\pi/6}^{\pi/4} \sec^2 x \, dx$ using Part 2 of the Fundamental Theorem of Calculus.

7. _____

8. (a) Graph the function $y = -0.3x^2 + 1.5x$ over the
  interval $[0, 6]$.
  (b) Integrate $y = -0.3x^2 + 1.5x$ over $[0, 6]$.
  (c) Find the area of the region between the graph in
  part (a) and the x-axis.

8. (a)

[0, 6] by [−2.25, 2.25]

(b) _____

(c) _____

9. (a) Let $f(x) = 3x + 2$. Find K so that
$$\int_2^x f(t)\, dt + K = \int_8^x f(t)\, dt.$$

  (b) Find $\dfrac{d}{dx}\displaystyle\int_{-1}^x f(t)\, dt.$

9. (a) _____

(b) _____

10. A particle moves along a
coordinate axis. Its position
at time t (sec) is
$s(t) = \displaystyle\int_0^t f(x)\, dx$ ft, where
f is the function whose
graph is shown.

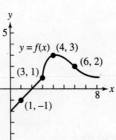

10. (a) _____

(b) _____

(c) _____

(d) _____

(e) _____

  (a) What is the particle's position at $t = 0$?
  (b) What is the particle's position at $t = 3$?
  (c) What is the particle's velocity at $t = 4$?
  (d) Approximately when is the acceleration zero?
  (e) At what time during the first 7 sec does s have
  its smallest value?

11. Use the Trapezoidal Rule with $n = 4$ to approximate
the value of $\displaystyle\int_1^5 (4 - x^2)\, dx.$

11. _____

12. A mural has the shape shown, where the
measurements shown were taken at 24-cm intervals.
Use Simpson's Rule to estimate the area of the mural.

12. _____

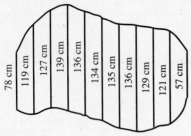

© Addison Wesley Longman, Inc.

Directions: Show all steps leading to your answers, including any intermediate results obtained using a graphing utility. Use the back of the test or another sheet of paper if necessary.

1. Write an equation for the line through $P(5, -3)$ that is
   (a) parallel to, and
   (b) perpendicular to the line $4x - 5y = 2$.

1. (a) _____
   (b) _____

2. Let $f(x) = 2 - |1 + x|$.
   (a) Draw the graph of $y = f(x)$.
   (b) Find the domain of f.
   (c) Find the range of f.

2. (a)

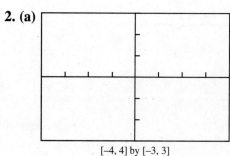

[–4, 4] by [–3, 3]

   (b) _____
   (c) _____

3. Let $g(x) = \dfrac{x^2}{1 + x^4}$. Which of the following words or phrases describe the function g?

   I. Odd   II. Even   III. One-to-one

   (A) I only   (B) II only   (C) III only
   (D) I and III   (E) II and III

3. _____

4. Determine how much time is required for an investment to quadruple (increase to 4 times the original amount) if interest is earned at a rate of 7.1% compounded continuously.

4. _____

5. A curve is parametrized by $x = t, y = \sqrt{t + 2}, t \geq -2$.
   (a) Graph the curve. Indicate the direction in which the curve is traced.
   (b) Write a Cartesian equation for a curve that contains the parametrized curve. What portion of the graph of the Cartesian equation is traced by the parametrized curve?

5. (a)

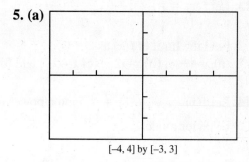

[–4, 4] by [–3, 3]

   (b) _____

6. Find a parametrization for the line segment with endpoints $(13, 5)$ and $(7, 8)$. (Remember to specify the parameter interval.)

6. _____

7. Let $f(x) = \dfrac{20}{1 + 3e^{-x}}$. Find a formula for $f^{-1}(x)$.

7. _____

8. Solve the equation algebraically.
   $1.08^x = 5$

8. _____

9. Let $g(x) = 2 \sec (3x - \pi) + 1$. Determine **(a)** the period,
   (b) the domain, and **(c)** the range, and **(d)** draw the graph
   of the function.

9. (a) _____
   (b) _____
   (c) _____
   (d)

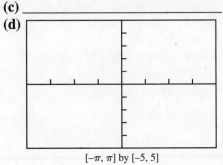

$[-\pi, \pi]$ by $[-5, 5]$

10. Solve the equation $\sin x = 0.2$ on the interval $0 \le x < 2\pi$.

10. _____

11. Which of the following statements are true about the
    function f whose graph is shown to the right?

11. _____

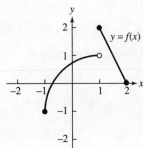

   I. $\lim\limits_{x \to -1^+} f(x) = -1$

   II. $f(1) = \lim\limits_{x \to 1} f(x)$

   III. $\lim\limits_{x \to 1^-} f(x) = 1$

   (A) I and II   (B) I and III   (C) II and III
   (D) I only   (E) I, II, and III

12. Determine $\lim\limits_{x \to 0} \left(\dfrac{\sin x}{2x} + 3x + 4 \right)$.

12. _____

13. Let $f(x) = \begin{cases} 5 - x^2, & x \le 2 \\ \dfrac{x + 3}{x - 2}, & x > 2 \end{cases}$.

   Find the limit of $f(x)$ as
   (a) $x \to -\infty$, **(b)** $x \to 2^-$, **(c)** $x \to 2^+$, and **(d)** $x \to \infty$.

13. (a) _____
    (b) _____
    (c) _____
    (d) _____

14. Let $f(x) = \dfrac{3x^5 - 2x^2 + 3}{2x^2 - 5}$. Find a power function end
   behavior model for f.

14. _____

15. Let $f(x) = \begin{cases} \dfrac{3x}{x + 4}, & x \le 4, x \ne -4 \\ \sqrt{x - 3}, & x > 4 \end{cases}$

15. _____

   Find the point(s) of discontinuity of the function f.
   Identify each type of discontinuity.

   _____

16. Let $f(x) = \dfrac{x^2 + 3x - 4}{x^2 - 4x + 3}$.

Give a formula for the extended function that is

continuous at $x = 1$.

16. _____

17. An object is dropped from a 75-ft cliff. Its height in feet above the beach after t sec is given by $h(t) = 75 - 16t^2$.
   (a) Find the average velocity during the interval from $t = 1$ to $t = 2$.
   (b) Find the instantaneous velocity at $t = 2$.

17. (a) _____
    (b) _____

18. Let $f(x) = \begin{cases} 3 - x^2, x \le 2 \\ 4x - 9, x > 2 \end{cases}$.

Determine whether the graph of $y = f(x)$ has a tangent at $x = 2$. If not, explain why not.

18. _____

_____

19. The graph of $y = g(x)$ shown here is made of line segments joined end to end. Graph the function's derivative.

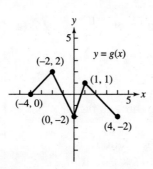

19.

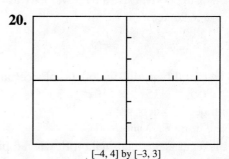

$[-4.7, 4.7]$ by $[-3.1, 3.1]$

20. The graph below shows the *derivative* of a continuous function f, where $f(0) = 1$. Sketch a possible graph of $y = f(x)$.

$y = f'(x)$

$[-4, 4]$ by $[-3, 3]$

20.

$[-4, 4]$ by $[-3, 3]$

21. Find all values of x for which the function $y = \dfrac{\sqrt{x}}{5x - 2}$ is differentiable.

21. _____

22. Let $f(x) = x^2 - |x - 4|$. Which of the following describes the behavior of f at $x = 4$?

   (A) differentiable   (B) corner
   (C) cusp   (D) vertical tangent
   (E) discontinuity

22. _____

23. Find $\dfrac{dy}{dx}$, where $y = \dfrac{(x + 2)(x + 4)}{x - 1}$.

23. _____

24. Find **(a)** $\dfrac{dy}{dx}$ and **(b)** $\dfrac{d^2y}{dx^2}$, where $y = x^4 - 5x^3 + 9x - 15$.

24. (a) _____

    (b) _____

25. A particle moves along a line so that its position at any
    time $t \geq 0$ is given by the function $s(t) = 2t^3 - 1.5t + 6$,
    where s is measured in meters and t is measured in
    minutes.
    (a) Find the displacement during the first 5 minutes.
    (b) Find the average velocity during the first 5 minutes.
    (c) Find the instantaneous velocity when $t = 5$ minutes.
    (d) Find the acceleration of the particle when
    $t = 5$ minutes.
    (e) At what value or values of t does the particle change
    direction?

25. (a) _____
    (b) _____
    (c) _____
    (d) _____
    (e) _____

26. The values of the coordinate s of a moving body for
    various values of t are given.

t (sec)	0	5	10	15	20	25	30	35
s (ft)	0.5	3	4.5	5	4.5	3	0.5	-3

    (a) Plot s versus t, and sketch a smooth curve through the
    given points.
    (b) Assuming this smooth curve represents the motion
    of the body, estimate the velocity at $t = 10$ sec and at
    $t = 25$ sec.

26. (a)
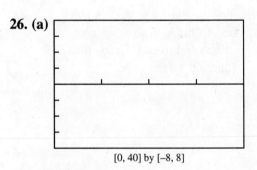
[0, 40] by [–8, 8]

    (b) $t = 10$: _____
        $t = 25$: _____

27. The monthly profit (in dollars) of a certain artist is given
    by $P(x) = -15x^3 + 150x^2 + 300x - 400$, where x is the
    number of pieces sold.
    (a) Graph $P(x)$ and $P'(x)$.
    (b) What is the marginal profit when 6 pieces are sold?
    (c) What is the profit when the marginal profit is
    greatest?
    (d) What is the maximum profit possible?
    (Assume x is an integer.)

27. (a)
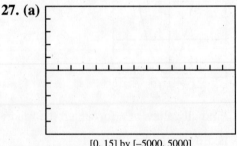
[0, 15] by [–5000, 5000]

    (b) _____
    (c) _____
    (d) _____

28. Find $\dfrac{dy}{dx}$ if $y = \dfrac{3 \tan x}{4 - \cos x}$.

28. _____

29. Find $\dfrac{dy}{dx}$ if $y = \sec(3x^2)$.

29. _____

30. Find $(f \circ g)'$ at $x = 4$ if $f(u) = u^3 - 5$ and $u = g(x) = 3\sqrt{x}$.

30. _____

A Chapters 1–4 (continued)   NAME

31. A curve is defined parametrically by $x = \sin 3t$, $y = \cos 3t$, $0 \le t \le 2\pi$. Find the equation of the line tangent to the curve at the point defined by $t = \dfrac{2\pi}{9}$.

31. _____

32. Use implicit differentiation to find $\dfrac{dy}{dx}$ if $\cos xy = 2x^2 - 3y$.

32. _____

33. Find $\dfrac{dy}{dx}$ if $y = \tan^{-1}(x - 4)$.

33. _____

34. Let $y = x^{\cos x}$. Use logarithmic differentiation to find $\dfrac{dy}{dx}$.

34. _____

    (A) $x^{-\sin x}(\cos x - \ln x)$ (B) $x^{\cos x}\left(\dfrac{\cos x}{x} - \ln x \sin x\right)$

    (C) $x^{-1+\cos x}\cos x$ (D) $x^{\cos x}\left(\dfrac{\cos x}{x} + \ln x \sin x\right)$

    (E) $\left(\dfrac{\cos x}{x} - \ln x \sin x\right)\cos x \ln x$

35. Find $\dfrac{dy}{dx}$ if $y = e^{2x} - \ln x^2$.

35. _____

36. Find the (global) extreme values and where they occur.

36. Min: _____ at $x =$ _____
     Max: _____ at $x =$ _____

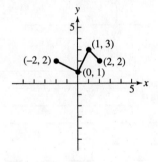

37. For $y = \dfrac{1}{4}x^4 - \dfrac{2}{3}x^3 + \dfrac{1}{2}x^2 - 3$ find the exact intervals on which the function is

    (a) increasing,   (b) decreasing,

    (c) concave up,   (d) concave down.

    Then find any

    (e) local extreme values,   (f) inflection points.

37. (a) _____
    (b) _____
    (c) _____
    (d) _____
    (e) Min: _____ at $x =$ _____
        Max: _____ at $x =$ _____
    (f) _____

_____

38. A car's odometer (mileage counter) reads exactly 59,024 miles at 8:00 A.M. and 59,094 miles at 10:00 A.M. Assuming the car's position and velocity functions are differentiable, what theorem can be used to show that the car was traveling at exactly 35 mph at some time between 8:00 A.M. and 10:00 A.M.?

   I. Intermediate Value Theorem for Derivatives
  II. Extreme Value Theorem
 III. Mean Value Theorem

  (A) I only   (B) II only   (C) III only
  (D) I and III   (E) II and III

38. _____

39. Find all possible functions with the derivative $f'(x) = 4x^2 - 3 + \sin x$.

39. _____

40. Sketch a possible graph of a continuous function f that has domain $[-3, 3]$, where $f(1) = -2$ and the graph of $y = f'(x)$ is shown below.

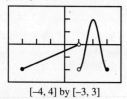

[–4, 4] by [–3, 3]

40.

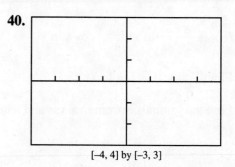

[–4, 4] by [–3, 3]

41. A piece of cardboard measures 22- by 35-in. Two equal squares are removed from the corners of a 22-in. side as shown in the figure. Two equal rectangles are removed from the other corners so that the tabs can be folded to form a rectangular box with a lid.
  (a) Write a formula $V(x)$ for the volume of the box.
  (b) Find the domain of V for the problem situation.
  (c) Find the maximum volume and the value of x that gives it.

41. (a) _____
  (b) Domain: _____
  (c) Volume: _____
      $x \approx$ _____

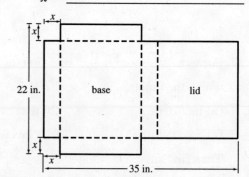

42. The function $f(x) = x^3 + ax^2 + bx$ has a local minimum at $x = 3$ and a point of inflection at $x = -1$. Find the values of a and b.

42. $a =$ _____
     $b =$ _____

Directions: Show all steps leading to your answers, including any intermediate results obtained using a graphing utility. Use the back of the test or another sheet of paper if necessary.

1. Write an equation for the line through $P(6, -2)$ that is
   (a) parallel to and
   (b) perpendicular to the line $3x + 4y = 2$.

1. **(a)** _____
   (b) _____

2. Let $f(x) = -1 + |x - 2|$.
   (a) Draw the graph of $y = f(x)$.
   (b) Find the domain of f.
   (c) Find the range of f.

2. **(a)**
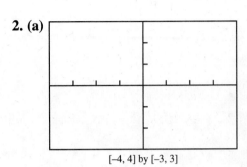
$[-4, 4]$ by $[-3, 3]$

   (b) _____
   (c) _____

3. Let $g(x) = \dfrac{3x^3 + x}{x^2 + 1}$. Which of the following words or phrases describe the function g?

   I. Odd   II. Even   III. One-to-one

   (A) I only   (B) II only   (C) III only
   (D) I and III   (E) II and III

3. _____

4. Determine how much time is required for an investment to quintuple (increase to 5 times the original amount) if interest is earned at a rate of 6.1% compounded continuously.

4. _____

5. A curve is parametrized by $x = t$, $y = \sqrt{3 - t}$, $t \le 3$.
   (a) Graph the curve. Indicate the direction in which the curve is traced.
   (b) Write a Cartesian equation for a curve that contains the parametrized curve. What portion of the graph of the Cartesian equation is traced by the parametrized curve?

5. **(a)**
$[-4, 4]$ by $[-3, 3]$

   (b) _____

6. Find a parametrization for the line segment with endpoints $(4, 11)$ and $(9, 3)$. (Remember to specify the parameter interval.)

6. _____

7. Let $f(x) = \dfrac{15}{5e^{-x} + 2}$. Find a formula for $f^{-1}(x)$.

7. _____

8. Solve the equation algebraically.
$1.06^x = 4$

8. _____

9. Let $g(x) = -2.5 \csc(2x - \pi) - 1.5$. Determine
(a) the period, **(b)** the domain, and **(c)** the range, and
(d) draw the graph of the function.

9. **(a)** _____
   (b) _____
   (c) _____
   (d)

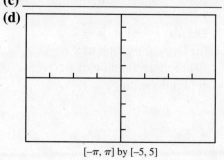

$[-\pi, \pi]$ by $[-5, 5]$

10. Solve the equation $\cos x = 0.6$ on the interval $0 \le x < 2\pi$.

10. _____

11. Which of the following statements are true about the
function f whose graph is shown to the right?

    I. $\lim\limits_{x \to -1^+} f(x) = 2$

    II. $\lim\limits_{x \to 1^-} f(x) = 0$

    III. $f(0) = \lim\limits_{x \to 0} f(x)$

    (A) I and II   (B) I and III   (C) II and III
    (D) I only   (E) I, II and III

11. _____

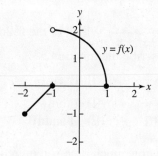

12. Determine $\lim\limits_{x \to 0} \left(\dfrac{\sin x}{5x} + 2x - 3 \right)$.

12. _____

13. Let $f(x) = \begin{cases} \dfrac{2x - 1}{x - 3}, & x < 3 \\ x^2 - 10, & x \ge 3 \end{cases}$.

Find the limit of $f(x)$ as
(a) $x \to -\infty$, **(b)** $x \to 3^-$, **(c)** $x \to 3^+$, and **(d)** $x \to \infty$.

13. **(a)** _____
   (b) _____
   (c) _____
   (d) _____

14. Let $f(x) = \dfrac{5x^6 - 2x^4 + 3x}{3x^4 + 18}$. Find a power function end
behavior model for f.

14. _____

15. Let $f(x) = \begin{cases} \dfrac{3x + 1}{x + 2}, & x < 3, x \ne -2 \\ \sqrt{x + 1}, & x \ge 3 \end{cases}$

Find the point(s) of discontinuity of the function f.
Identify each type of discontinuity.

15. _____

_____

16. Let $f(x) = \dfrac{x^2 + x - 2}{x^2 + 7x + 10}$.

Give a formula for the extended function that is

continuous at $x = -2$.

16. _____

17. An object is dropped from a 195-ft tower. Its height in feet
above the street after t sec is given by $h(t) = 195 - 16t^2$.
 (a) Find the average velocity during the interval from
   $t = 1$ to $t = 3$.
 (b) Find the instantaneous velocity at $t = 3$.

17. (a) _____
    (b) _____

18. Let $f(x) = \begin{cases} 2x - 5, & x \le 1 \\ x^2 - 6, & x > 1 \end{cases}$.

Determine whether the graph of $y = f(x)$ has a tangent
at $x = 1$. If not, explain why not.

18. _____
    _____

19. The graph of $y = g(x)$ shown
here is made of line segments
joined end to end. Graph the
function's derivative.

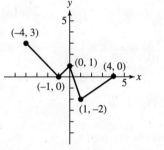

19.

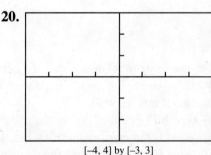

[–4.7, 4.7] by [–3.1, 3.1]

20. The graph below shows the *derivative* of a continuous
function f, where $f(0) = -1$. Sketch a possible graph of
$y = f(x)$.

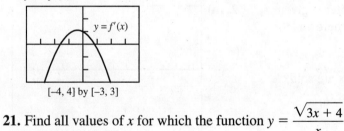

[–4, 4] by [–3, 3]

20.

[–4, 4] by [–3, 3]

21. Find all values of x for which the function $y = \dfrac{\sqrt{3x + 4}}{x}$
is differentiable.

21. _____

22. Let $f(x) = x^3 + \sqrt[3]{x - 3}$. Which of the following
describes the behavior of f at $x = 3$?

 (A) differentiable   (B) corner
 (C) cusp   (D) vertical tangent
 (E) discontinuity

22. _____

23. Find $\dfrac{dy}{dx}$, where $y = \dfrac{(x - 2)(x + 3)}{x + 4}$.

23. _____

24. Find **(a)** $\dfrac{dy}{dx}$ and **(b)** $\dfrac{d^2y}{dx^2}$, where $y = x^5 + 8x^3 - 2x^2 + 5$.

24. **(a)** _____

(b) _____

25. A particle moves along a line so that its position at any time $t \geq 0$ is given by the function $s(t) = -t^3 + t^2 + 5t + 3$, where s is measured in meters and t is measured in minutes.
   (a) Find the displacement during the first 4 minutes.
   (b) Find the average velocity during the first 4 minutes.
   (c) Find the instantaneous velocity when $t = 4$ minutes.
   (d) Find the acceleration of the particle when $t = 4$ minutes.
   (e) At what value or values of t does the particle change direction?

25. **(a)** _____
(b) _____
(c) _____
(d) _____
(e) _____

26. The values of the coordinate s of a moving body for various values of t are given.

t (sec)	0	2	4	6	8	10	12	14
s (ft)	-5	-11.5	-15	-15.5	-13	-7.5	1	12.5

   (a) Plot s versus t, and sketch a smooth curve through the given points.
   (b) Assuming this smooth curve represents the motion of the body, estimate the velocity at $t = 2$ sec and at $t = 12$ sec.

26. **(a)**

[0, 16] by [–20, 20]

(b) $t = 2$: _____
$t = 12$: _____

27. The monthly profit (in dollars) of a certain writer is given by $P(x) = -20x^3 + 200x^2 + 200x - 1500$, where x is the number of articles sold.
   (a) Graph $P(x)$ and $P'(x)$.
   (b) What is the marginal profit when 4 articles are sold?
   (c) What is the profit when the marginal profit is greatest?
   (d) What is the maximum profit possible? (Assume x is an integer.)

27. **(a)**

[0, 15] by [–5000, 5000]

(b) _____
(c) _____
(d) _____

28. Find $\dfrac{dy}{dx}$ if $y = \dfrac{2 \sin x}{5 - \sec x}$.

28. _____

29. Find $\dfrac{dy}{dx}$ if $y = \tan (4x^3)$.

29. _____

30. Find $(f \circ g)'$ at $x = 9$ if $f(u) = 4u^2 + 3$ and $u = g(x) = 4\sqrt{x}$.

30. _____

31. A curve is defined parametrically by $x = \cos 2t$,
$y = \sin 4t$, $0 \le t \le 2\pi$. Find the equation of the line
tangent to the curve at the point defined by $t = \dfrac{\pi}{12}$.

31. _____

32. Use implicit differentiation to find $\dfrac{dy}{dx}$ if $\sin xy = 5x + 3y^2$.

32. _____

33. Find $\dfrac{dy}{dx}$ if $y = \sec^{-1}(x + 3)$.

33. _____

34. Let $y = (\sin x)^x$. Use logarithmic differentiation to find $\dfrac{dy}{dx}$.

34. _____

(A) $x(\sin x)^{x-1}$ (B) $(\cos x)^x + \sin x \ln x$

(C) $(\sin x)^x \ln(\sin x)$ (D) $(\sin x)^x[x \cot x + \ln(\sin x)]$

(E) $(\sin x)^x[\ln(\sin x) - x \cot x]$

35. Find $\dfrac{dy}{dx}$ if $y = \ln 4x - e^{(x^2)}$.

35. _____

36. Find the (global) extreme values and where they occur.

36. Min: _____ at $x =$ _____

Max: _____ at $x =$ _____

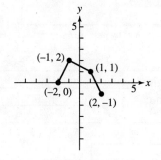

37. For $y = -\dfrac{1}{4}x^4 - \dfrac{1}{3}x^3 + 2x$ find the exact intervals on
which the function is

(a) increasing,   **(b)** decreasing,

(c) concave up,   **(d)** concave down.

Then find any

(e) local extreme values,   **(f)** inflection points.

37. (a) _____

(b) _____

(c) _____

(d) _____

(e) Min: _____ at $x =$ _____

Max: _____ at $x =$ _____

(f) _____

38. An airplane traveling toward Denver is 642 miles away
    at 1:30 P.M. and 42 miles away at 3:00 P.M. Assuming
    the plane's position and velocity functions are
    differentiable, which of the following can be used to show
    that the plane was traveling at exactly 400 mph at some time
    between 1:30 P.M. and 3:00 P.M.?
    I. Extreme Value Theorem
    II. Mean Value Theorem
    III. Intermediate Value Theorem for Derivatives

    (A) I only   (B) II only   (C) III only
    (D) Either I or III (E) Either II or III

38. _____

39. Find all possible functions with the derivative
    $f'(x) = 5x + 4 - \cos x$.

39. _____

40. Sketch a possible graph of a continuous function f that
    has domain $[-3, 3]$, where $f(1) = 2$ and the graph of
    $y = f'(x)$ is shown below.

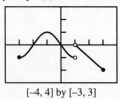

[−4, 4] by [−3, 3]

40.

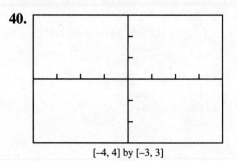

[−4, 4] by [−3, 3]

41. A piece of cardboard measures 20- by 36-in. Two equal
    squares are removed from the corners of a 20-in. side as
    shown in the figure. Two equal rectangles are removed
    from the other corners so that the tabs can be folded to
    form a rectangular box with a lid.
    (a) Write a formula $V(x)$ for the volume of the box.
    (b) Find the domain of V for the problem situation.
    (c) Find the maximum volume and the value of x that
        gives it.

41. (a) _____
    (b) Domain: _____
    (c) Volume: _____
        $x \approx$ _____

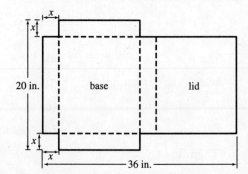

42. The function $f(x) = ax^3 + 12x^2 + bx$ has a local
    maximum at $x = 5$ and a point of inflection at $x = 2$.
    Find the values of a and b.

42. $a =$ _____
    $b =$ _____

Directions: Show all steps leading to your answers, including any intermediate results obtained using a graphing utility. Use the back of the test or another sheet of paper if necessary.

1. Write an equation for the line through $P(5, -3)$ that is
 (a) parallel to, and
 (b) perpendicular to the line $4x - 5y = 2$.

1. (a) _____
   (b) _____

2. Let $f(x) = 2 - |1 + x|$.
 (a) Draw the graph of $y = f(x)$.
 (b) Find the domain of f.
 (c) Find the range of f.

2. (a)

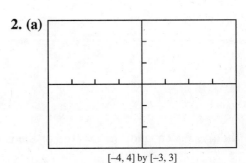

[−4, 4] by [−3, 3]

 (b) _____
 (c) _____

3. Let $g(x) = \dfrac{x^2}{1 + x^4}$. Which of the following words or phrases describe the function g?

   I. Odd   II. Even   III. One-to-one

   (A) I only   (B) II only   (C) III only
   (D) I and III   (E) II and III

3. _____

4. Determine how much time is required for an investment to quadruple (increase to 4 times the original amount) if interest is earned at a rate of 7.1% compounded continuously.

4. _____

5. A curve is parametrized by $x = t,\ y = \sqrt{t + 2},\ t \geq -2$.
 (a) Graph the curve. Indicate the direction in which the curve is traced.
 (b) Write a Cartesian equation for a curve that contains the parametrized curve. What portion of the graph of the Cartesian equation is traced by the parametrized curve?

5. (a)

[−4, 4] by [−3, 3]

 (b) _____

6. Find a parametrization for the line segment with endpoints $(13, 5)$ and $(7, 8)$. (Remember to specify the parameter interval.)

6. _____

7. Let $f(x) = \dfrac{20}{1 + 3e^{-x}}$. Find a formula for $f^{-1}(x)$.

7. _____

8. Let $g(x) = 2 \sec (3x - \pi) + 1$. Determine **(a)** the period, **(b)** the domain, and **(c)** the range, and **(d)** draw the graph of the function.

8. (a) _____
(b) _____
(c) _____
(d)

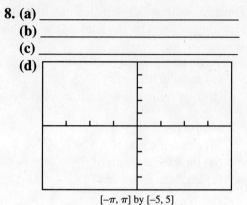

$[-\pi, \pi]$ by $[-5, 5]$

9. Solve the equation $\sin x = 0.2$ on the interval $0 \le x < 2\pi$.

9. _____

10. Which of the following statements are true about the function f whose graph is shown to the right?

10. _____

   I. $\lim\limits_{x \to -1^+} f(x) = -1$

   II. $f(1) = \lim\limits_{x \to 1} f(x)$

   III. $\lim\limits_{x \to 1^-} f(x) = 1$

   (A) I and II   (B) I and III   (C) II and III
   (D) I only   (E) I, II, and III

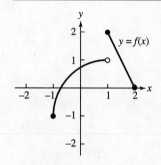

11. Determine $\lim\limits_{x \to 0} \left(\dfrac{\sin x}{2x} + 3x + 4 \right)$.

11. _____

12. Let $f(x) = \begin{cases} 5 - x^2, & x \le 2 \\ \dfrac{x + 3}{x - 2}, & x > 2 \end{cases}$.

Find the limit of $f(x)$ as
(a) $x \to -\infty$, **(b)** $x \to 2^-$, **(c)** $x \to 2^+$, and **(d)** $x \to \infty$.

12. (a) _____
(b) _____
(c) _____
(d) _____

13. Let $f(x) = \dfrac{x^2 + 3x - 4}{x^2 - 4x + 3}$.

Give a formula for the extended function that is

continuous at $x = 1$.

13. _____

14. An object is dropped from a 75-ft cliff. Its height in feet above the beach after t sec is given by $h(t) = 75 - 16t^2$.
   (a) Find the average velocity during the interval from $t = 1$ to $t = 2$.
   (b) Find the instantaneous velocity at $t = 2$.

14. (a) _____
(b) _____

15. Let $f(x) = \begin{cases} 3 - x^2, & x \le 2 \\ 4x - 9, & x > 2 \end{cases}$.

Determine whether the graph of $y = f(x)$ has a tangent at $x = 2$. If not, explain why not.

15. _____

_____

16. The graph of $y = g(x)$ shown here is made of line segments joined end to end. Graph the function's derivative.

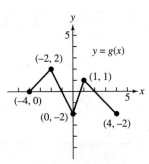

16.

[–4.7, 4.7] by [–3.1, 3.1]

17. Find all values of x for which the function $y = \dfrac{\sqrt{x}}{5x - 2}$ is differentiable.

17. _____

18. Let $f(x) = x^2 - |x - 4|$. Which of the following describes the behavior of f at $x = 4$?

  (A) differentiable   (B) corner
  (C) cusp   (D) vertical tangent
  (E) discontinuity

18. _____

19. Find $\dfrac{dy}{dx}$, where $y = \dfrac{(x + 2)(x + 4)}{x - 1}$.

19. _____

20. Find **(a)** $\dfrac{dy}{dx}$ and **(b)** $\dfrac{d^2y}{dx^2}$, where $y = x^4 - 5x^3 + 9x - 15$.

20. (a) _____

    (b) _____

21. The monthly profit (in dollars) of a certain artist is given by $P(x) = -15x^3 + 150x^2 + 300x - 400$, where x is the number of pieces sold.
  (a) Graph $P(x)$ and $P'(x)$.
  (b) What is the marginal profit when 6 pieces are sold?
  (c) What is the profit when the marginal profit is greatest?
  (d) What is the maximum profit possible?
      (Assume x is an integer.)

21. (a)

[0, 15] by [–5000, 5000]

    (b) _____
    (c) _____
    (d) _____

22. Find $\dfrac{dy}{dx}$ if $y = \dfrac{3 \tan x}{4 - \cos x}$.

22. _____

23. Find $\dfrac{dy}{dx}$ if $y = \sec (3x^2)$.

23. _____

24. Find $(f \circ g)'$ at $x = 4$ if $f(u) = u^3 - 5$ and $u = g(x) = 3\sqrt{x}$.

24. _____

25. A curve is defined parametrically by $x = \sin 3t$, $y = \cos 3t$, $0 \le t \le 2\pi$. Find the equation of the line tangent to the curve at the point defined by $t = \dfrac{2\pi}{9}$.

25. _____

26. Use implicit differentiation to find $\dfrac{dy}{dx}$ if $\cos xy = 2x^2 - 3y$.

26. _____

27. Find $\dfrac{dy}{dx}$ if $y = \tan^{-1}(x - 4)$.

27. _____

28. Let $y = x^{\cos x}$. Use logarithmic differentiation to find $\dfrac{dy}{dx}$.

28. _____

    (A) $x^{-\sin x}(\cos x - \ln x)$ (B) $x^{\cos x}\left(\dfrac{\cos x}{x} - \ln x \sin x\right)$

    (C) $x^{-1+\cos x}\cos x$ (D) $x^{\cos x}\left(\dfrac{\cos x}{x} + \ln x \sin x\right)$

    (E) $\left(\dfrac{\cos x}{x} - \ln x \sin x\right)\cos x \ln x$

29. Find $\dfrac{dy}{dx}$ if $y = e^{2x} - \ln x^2$.

29. _____

30. Find the (global) extreme values and where they occur.

30. Min: _____ at $x =$ _____

       Max: _____ at $x =$ _____

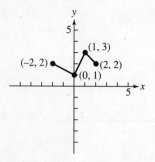

31. For $y = \dfrac{1}{4}x^4 - \dfrac{2}{3}x^3 + \dfrac{1}{2}x^2 - 3$ find the exact intervals on which the function is

    (a) increasing,   (b) decreasing,

    (c) concave up,   (d) concave down.

    Then find any

    (e) local extreme values,   (f) inflection points.

31. (a) _____

    (b) _____

    (c) _____

    (d) _____

    (e) Min: _____ at $x =$ _____

         Max: _____ at $x =$ _____

    (f) _____

32. A car's odometer (mileage counter) reads exactly 59,024 miles at 8:00 A.M. and 59,094 miles at 10:00 A.M. Assuming the car's position and velocity functions are differentiable, what theorem can be used to show that the car was traveling at exactly 35 mph at some time between 8:00 A.M. and 10:00 A.M.?

32. _____

    I. Intermediate Value Theorem for Derivatives
    II. Extreme Value Theorem
    III. Mean Value Theorem

    (A) I only   (B) II only   (C) III only
    (D) I and III   (E) II and III

33. Find all possible functions with the derivative
$f'(x) = 4x^2 - 3 + \sin x$.

33. _____

34. Sketch a possible graph of a continuous function f that
has domain $[-3, 3]$, where $f(1) = -2$ and the graph of
$y = f'(x)$ is shown below.

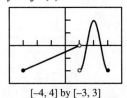

[–4, 4] by [–3, 3]

34.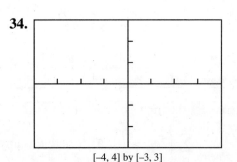

[–4, 4] by [–3, 3]

35. A piece of cardboard measures 22- by 35-in. Two equal
squares are removed from the corners of a 22-in. side as
shown in the figure. Two equal rectangles are removed
from the other corners so that the tabs can be folded to
form a rectangular box with a lid.
  (a) Write a formula $V(x)$ for the volume of the box.
  (b) Find the domain of V for the problem situation.
  (c) Find the maximum volume and the value of x that
      gives it.

35. (a) _____
  (b) Domain: _____
  (c) Volume: _____
      $x \approx$ _____

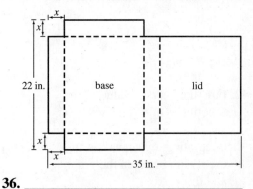

36. Find the linearization $L(x)$ of $f(x) = 3x^4 - 5x^3$ at $x = 2$.

  (A) $L(x) = 8x - 8$ (B) $L(x) = 32x - 56$
  (C) $L(x) = 36x$ (D) $L(x) = 36x + 8$
  (E) $L(x) = 36x - 64$

36. _____

37. You are using Newton's method to solve $\ln x - 3 = 0$.
If your first guess is $x_1 = 15$, what value will you calculate
for the next approximation x_2?

37. _____

38. Suppose that the edge lengths x, y, and z of a closed
rectangular box are changing at the following rates:
$\frac{dx}{dt} = 4$ ft/sec, $\frac{dy}{dt} = 0$ ft/sec, $\frac{dz}{dt} = -3$ ft/sec.

Find the rates at which the box's **(a)** volume,
(b) surface area, and **(c)** diagonal length
$s = \sqrt{x^2 + y^2 + z^2}$ are changing at the instant when
$x = 10$ ft, $y = 8$ ft, and $z = 5$ ft.

38. (a) _____
  (b) _____
  (c) _____

39. The table below shows the velocity of a car in an amusement park ride during the first 24 seconds of the ride. Use the left-endpoint values (LRAM) to estimate the distance traveled, using 6 intervals of length 4.

39. _____

Time (sec)	0	4	8	12	16	20	24
Velocity (ft/sec)	0	4	7	7	11	16	18

40. Express the limit as a definite integral.

$$\lim_{\|P\|\to 0} \sum_{k=1}^{n} \left(2c_k + \frac{1}{c_k^2}\right) \Delta x,$$ where P is any partition of $[7, 15]$.

40. _____

41. Suppose that f and g are continuous and that $\int_{-1}^{4} f(x)\, dx = 5$, $\int_{-1}^{4} g(x)\, dx = -2$, and $\int_{1}^{4} g(x)\, dx = 3$. Find each integral.

(a) $\int_{-1}^{4} [f(x) - g(x)]\, dx$ (b) $\int_{-1}^{4} [3f(x) + 5g(x)]\, dx$

(c) $\int_{-1}^{1} g(x)\, dx$

41. (a) _____

(b) _____

(c) _____

42. Find the average value of the function $g(x) = 2 + \sqrt{9 - x^2}$ on the interval $[-3, 3]$ without integrating, by appealing to the region between the graph and the x-axis.

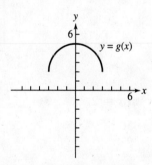

42. _____

43. Use NINT to evaluate $\int_{-1.7}^{2.6} \frac{5 \cos x}{e^x + x^2}\, dx$.

43. _____

44. Evaluate each integral using Part 2 of the Fundamental Theorem of Calculus.

(a) $\int_{-1}^{3} (3x^2 - 12x + 4)\, dx$ (b) $\int_{1}^{16} x^{3/4}\, dx$

(c) $\int_{\pi/2}^{5\pi/6} \csc\theta \cot\theta\, d\theta$

44. (a) _____

(b) _____

(c) _____

45. Find $\dfrac{dy}{dx}$ if $y = \int_{1}^{x^2} (3t^2 - 5t)\, dt$.

(A) $3x^2 - 5x$ (B) $6x^3 - 10x^2$ (C) $12x^3 - 10x$
(D) $6x^5 - 10x^3$ (E) $3x^6 - 5x^4$

45. _____

46. Use the Trapezoidal Rule with $n = 6$ to approximate the value of $\int_{0}^{3} e^x\, dx$

46. _____

Directions: Show all steps leading to your answers, including any intermediate results obtained using a graphing utility. Use the back of the test or another sheet of paper if necessary.

1. Write an equation for the line through $P(6, -2)$ that is
   (a) parallel to and
   (b) perpendicular to the line $3x + 4y = 2$.

1. **(a)** _____
   (b) _____

2. Let $f(x) = -1 + |x - 2|$.
   (a) Draw the graph of $y = f(x)$.
   (b) Find the domain of f.
   (c) Find the range of f.

2. **(a)**

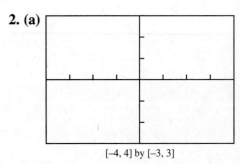

[−4, 4] by [−3, 3]

   (b) _____
   (c) _____

3. Let $g(x) = \dfrac{3x^3 + x}{x^2 + 1}$. Which of the following words or phrases describe the function g?

3. _____

   I. Odd   II. Even   III. One-to-one

   (A) I only   (B) II only   (C) III only
   (D) I and III   (E) II and III

4. Determine how much time is required for an investment to quintuple (increase to 5 times the original amount) if interest is earned at a rate of 6.1% compounded continuously.

4. _____

5. A curve is parametrized by $x = t$, $y = \sqrt{3 - t}$, $t \le 3$.
   (a) Graph the curve. Indicate the direction in which the curve is traced.
   (b) Write a Cartesian equation for a curve that contains the parametrized curve. What portion of the graph of the Cartesian equation is traced by the parametrized curve?

5. **(a)**

[−4, 4] by [−3, 3]

   (b) _____

6. Find a parametrization for the line segment with endpoints $(4, 11)$ and $(9, 3)$. (Remember to specify the parameter interval.)

6. _____

7. Let $f(x) = \dfrac{15}{5e^{-x} + 2}$. Find a formula for $f^{-1}(x)$.

7. _____

8. Let $g(x) = -2.5 \csc(2x - \pi) - 1.5$. Determine
(a) the period, (b) the domain, and (c) the range, and
(d) draw the graph of the function.

8. (a) _____

(b) _____

(c) _____

(d)

$[-\pi, \pi]$ by $[-5, 5]$

9. Solve the equation $\cos x = 0.6$ on the interval $0 \leq x < 2\pi$.

9. _____

10. Which of the following statements are true about the
function f whose graph is shown to the right?

   I. $\lim\limits_{x \to -1^+} f(x) = 2$

   II. $\lim\limits_{x \to 1^-} f(x) = 0$

   III. $f(0) = \lim\limits_{x \to 0} f(x)$

  (A) I and II   (B) I and III   (C) II and III
  (D) I only   (E) I, II and III

10. _____

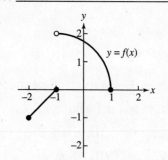

11. Determine $\lim\limits_{x \to 0} \left(\dfrac{\sin x}{5x} + 2x - 3 \right)$.

11. _____

12. Let $f(x) = \begin{cases} \dfrac{2x - 1}{x - 3}, & x < 3 \\ x^2 - 10, & x \geq 3 \end{cases}$.

Find the limit of $f(x)$ as
(a) $x \to -\infty$, (b) $x \to 3^-$, (c) $x \to 3^+$, and (d) $x \to \infty$.

12. (a) _____

(b) _____

(c) _____

(d) _____

13. Let $f(x) = \dfrac{x^2 + x - 2}{x^2 + 7x + 10}$.

Give a formula for the extended function that is

continuous at $x = -2$.

13. _____

14. An object is dropped from a 195-ft tower. Its height in feet
above the street after t sec is given by $h(t) = 195 - 16t^2$.
(a) Find the average velocity during the interval from
$t = 1$ to $t = 3$.
(b) Find the instantaneous velocity at $t = 3$.

14. (a) _____

(b) _____

15. Let $f(x) = \begin{cases} 2x - 5, & x \leq 1 \\ x^2 - 6, & x > 1 \end{cases}$.

Determine whether the graph of $y = f(x)$ has a tangent
at $x = 1$. If not, explain why not.

15. _____

_____

16. The graph of $y = g(x)$ shown here is made of line segments joined end to end. Graph the function's derivative.

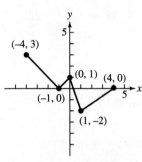

(–4, 3)
y
5
(0, 1) (4, 0)
(–1, 0)
5 x
(1, –2)

16.

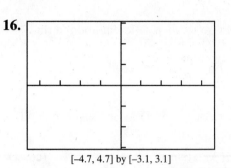

[–4.7, 4.7] by [–3.1, 3.1]

17. Find all values of x for which the function $y = \dfrac{\sqrt{3x + 4}}{x}$ is differentiable.

17. _____

18. Let $f(x) = x^3 + \sqrt[3]{x - 3}$. Which of the following describes the behavior of f at $x = 3$?

(A) differentiable   (B) corner
(C) cusp   (D) vertical tangent
(E) discontinuity

18. _____

19. Find $\dfrac{dy}{dx}$, where $y = \dfrac{(x - 2)(x + 3)}{x + 4}$.

19. _____

20. Find **(a)** $\dfrac{dy}{dx}$ and **(b)** $\dfrac{d^2y}{dx^2}$, where $y = x^5 + 8x^3 - 2x^2 + 5$.

20. (a) _____

(b) _____

21. The monthly profit (in dollars) of a certain writer is given by $P(x) = -20x^3 + 200x^2 + 200x - 1500$, where x is the number of articles sold.
(a) Graph $P(x)$ and $P'(x)$.
(b) What is the marginal profit when 4 articles are sold?
(c) What is the profit when the marginal profit is greatest?
(d) What is the maximum profit possible? (Assume x is an integer.)

21. (a)

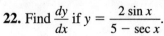

[0, 15] by [–5000, 5000]

(b) _____
(c) _____
(d) _____

22. Find $\dfrac{dy}{dx}$ if $y = \dfrac{2 \sin x}{5 - \sec x}$.

22. _____

23. Find $\dfrac{dy}{dx}$ if $y = \tan(4x^3)$.

23. _____

24. Find $(f \circ g)'$ at $x = 9$ if $f(u) = 4u^2 + 3$ and $u = g(x) = 4\sqrt{x}$.

24. _____

25. A curve is defined parametrically by $x = \cos 2t$, $y = \sin 4t$, $0 \le t \le 2\pi$. Find the equation of the line tangent to the curve at the point defined by $t = \dfrac{\pi}{12}$.

25. _____

26. Use implicit differentiation to find $\dfrac{dy}{dx}$ if $\sin xy = 5x + 3y^2$.   26. _____

27. Find $\dfrac{dy}{dx}$ if $y = \sec^{-1}(x + 3)$.   27. _____

28. Let $y = (\sin x)^x$. Use logarithmic differentiation to find $\dfrac{dy}{dx}$.   28. _____

   (A) $x(\sin x)^{x-1}$ (B) $(\cos x)^x + \sin x \ln x$

   (C) $(\sin x)^x \ln(\sin x)$ (D) $(\sin x)^x[x \cot x + \ln(\sin x)]$

   (E) $(\sin x)^x[\ln(\sin x) - x \cot x]$

29. Find $\dfrac{dy}{dx}$ if $y = \ln 4x - e^{(x^2)}$.   29. _____

30. Find the (global) extreme values and where they occur.   30. Min: _____ at $x =$ _____

                                                          Max: _____ at $x =$ _____

31. For $y = -\dfrac{1}{4}x^4 - \dfrac{1}{3}x^3 + 2x$ find the exact intervals on which the function is

   (a) increasing,   (b) decreasing,

   (c) concave up,   (d) concave down.

   Then find any

   (e) local extreme values,   (f) inflection points.

31. (a) _____

    (b) _____

    (c) _____

    (d) _____

    (e) Min: _____ at $x =$ _____

            Max: _____ at $x =$ _____

    (f) _____

32. An airplane traveling toward Denver is 642 miles away at 1:30 P.M. and 42 miles away at 3:00 P.M. Assuming the plane's position and velocity functions are differentiable, which of the following can be used to show that the plane was traveling at exactly 400 mph at some time between 1:30 P.M. and 3:00 P.M.?   32. _____

    I. Extreme Value Theorem

    II. Mean Value Theorem

    III. Intermediate Value Theorem for Derivatives

   (A) I only   (B) II only   (C) III only
   (D) Either I or III   (E) Either II or III

33. Find all possible functions with the derivative
$f'(x) = 5x + 4 - \cos x$.

33. _____

34. Sketch a possible graph of a continuous function f that
has domain $[-3, 3]$, where $f(1) = 2$ and the graph of
$y = f'(x)$ is shown below.

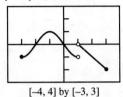

[–4, 4] by [–3, 3]

34.
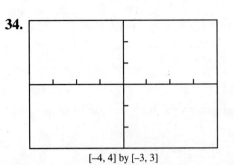

[–4, 4] by [–3, 3]

35. A piece of cardboard measures 20- by 36-in. Two equal
squares are removed from the corners of a 20-in. side as
shown in the figure. Two equal rectangles are removed
from the other corners so that the tabs can be folded to
form a rectangular box with a lid.
 (a) Write a formula $V(x)$ for the volume of the box.
 (b) Find the domain of V for the problem situation.
 (c) Find the maximum volume and the value of x that
 gives it.

35. (a) _____
  (b) Domain: _____
  (c) Volume: _____
  $x \approx$ _____

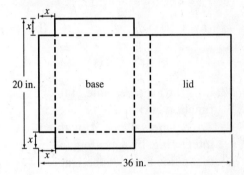

36. Find the linearization $L(x)$ of $f(x) = 2x^4 - 40x^2 + 100$
at $x = 3$.

 (A) $L(x) = -24x$ (B) $L(x) = -24x - 26$
 (C) $L(x) = -24x - 98$ (D) $L(x) = -98x$
 (E) $L(x) = -21x - 35$

36. _____

37. You are using Newton's method to solve $e^x - 2$.
If your first guess is $x_1 = 1$, what value will you calculate
for the next approximation x_2?

37. _____

38. Suppose that the edge lengths x, y, and z of a closed
rectangular box are changing at the following rates:
$\frac{dx}{dt} = 2$ ft/sec, $\frac{dy}{dt} = -5$ ft/sec, $\frac{dz}{dt} = 0$ ft/sec.

Find the rates at which the box's **(a)** volume,
(b) surface area, and **(c)** diagonal length
$s = \sqrt{x^2 + y^2 + z^2}$ are changing at the instant when
$x = 7$ ft, $y = 4$ ft, and $z = 9$ ft.

38. (a) _____
  (b) _____
  (c) _____

39. The table below shows the velocity of a running dog during a 35-second time interval. Use the right-endpoint values (RRAM) to estimate the distance traveled, using 7 intervals of length 5.

39. _____

Time (sec)	0	5	10	15	20	25	30	35
Velocity (ft/sec)	18	22	28	27	25	26	28	30

40. Express the limit as a definite integral.

$$\lim_{\|P\|\to 0} \sum_{k=1}^{n} \left(5c_k^2 - \frac{3}{c_k}\right) \Delta x,$$ where P is any partition of $[3, 11]$.

40. _____

41. Suppose that f and g are continuous and that $\int_{-2}^{5} f(x)\,dx = 3$, $\int_{-2}^{3} f(x)\,dx = 7$, and $\int_{-2}^{3} g(x)\,dx = -8$. Find each integral.

(a) $\int_{3}^{5} f(x)\,dx$ (b) $\int_{-2}^{3} [f(x) + g(x)]\,dx$

(c) $\int_{-2}^{3} [4g(x) - 5f(x)]\,dx$

41. (a) _____

(b) _____

(c) _____

42. Find the average value of the function $g(x) = 5 - \sqrt{16 - x^2}$ on the interval $[-4, 4]$ without integrating, by appealing to the region between the graph and the x-axis.

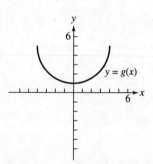

42. _____

43. Use NINT to evaluate $\int_{-5.2}^{1.2} \frac{2e^x}{x^2 + \cos x}\,dx$.

43. _____

44. Evaluate each integral using Part 2 of the Fundamental Theorem of Calculus.

(a) $\int_{-2}^{4} (5x^2 + 14x - 3)\,dx$ (b) $\int_{1}^{8} x^{2/3}\,dx$

(c) $\int_{\pi/3}^{2\pi/3} \csc^2\theta\,d\theta$

44. (a) _____

(b) _____

(c) _____

45. Find $\dfrac{dy}{dx}$ if $y = \int_{1}^{x^3} (6t^2 - 7)\,dt$.

(A) $18x^4 - 21x^2$ (B) $12x^5 - 7x^3$ (C) $12x^5 - 21x^2$
(D) $6x^6 - 7$ (E) $18x^8 - 21x^2$

45. _____

46. Use the Trapezoidal Rule with $n = 6$ to approximate the value of $\int_{2}^{4} 5 \ln x\,dx$.

46. _____

1. Evaluate the integral $\int (x^{-2} + 6x^2)\, dx$.

   (A) $-2x^{-3} + 12x + C$ (B) $-x^{-1} + 2x^3 + C$

   (C) $-\frac{1}{3}x^{-3} + 2x^3 + C$ (D) $-\frac{1}{2}x^{-1} + 3x^3 + C$

   (E) $-\frac{1}{2}x^{-3} + 3x + C$

1. _____

2. Solve the initial value problem.
   Support your answer by overlaying your solution on a
   slope field for the differential equation.

   $\frac{dy}{dx} = 3x^2 - 2$

   $y(-1) = 2$

2. _____

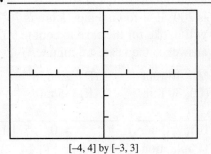

[−4, 4] by [−3, 3]

3. Which u-substitution would be useful in evaluating
   $\int \sec^2 (3x - 2)\, dx$?

   (A) $u = \tan x$ (B) $u = \sec x$ (C) $u = 3x - 2$

   (D) $u = \sec^2 x$ (E) $u = \cos (3x - 2)$

3. _____

4. Use a u-substitution to evaluate $\int_0^{\pi/3} \cos^4 x \sin x\, dx$.

   (A) $-\frac{31}{160}$ (B) $\frac{59}{320}$ (C) $\frac{31}{160}$

   (D) $\frac{1}{5} - \frac{9\sqrt{3}}{160}$ (E) $\frac{9\sqrt{3}}{160} - \frac{1}{5}$

5. _____

5. Which of the following expressions is equivalent to
   $\int x^8 e^{2x}\, dx$? (*Hint:* Apply integration by parts once.)

   (A) $x^8 e^{2x} - \int 8x^7 e^{2x}\, dx$ (B) $0.5x^8 e^{2x} + \int 4x^7 e^{2x}\, dx$

   (C) $8x^7 e^{2x} + \int x^8 e^{2x}\, dx$ (D) $0.5x^8 e^{2x} - \int 4x^7 e^{2x}\, dx$

   (E) $-0.5x^8 e^{2x} - \int 4x^7 e^{2x}\, dx$

7. _____

6. Use tabular integration or repeated integration by parts to
   evaluate $\int x^2 \sin 0.5x\, dx$.

   (A) $(-2x^2 + 16) \cos 0.5x + 8x \sin 0.5x + C$
   (B) $(-2x^2 - 16) \cos 0.5x + 8x \sin 0.5x + C$
   (C) $(2x^2 - 16) \cos 0.5x + 8x \sin 0.5x + C$
   (D) $(-2x^2 + 16) \cos 0.5x - 8x \sin 0.5x + C$
   (E) $8x \cos 0.5x + (x^2 + 16) \sin 0.5x + C$

8. _____

1. Suppose the decay equation for a radioactive element is known to be $y = y_0 e^{-0.24t}$, with t in years. About how long will it take for of a sample of this element to decay to 70% of its original amount?

   (A) 0.85 yr   (B) 1.23 yr   (C) 1.37 yr
   (D) 1.49 yr   (E) 1.65 yr

1. _____

2. The temperature of a cake was 350° F at the instant it came out of the oven. After 10 minutes, its temperature is 200° F. If room temperature is 70° F, how much longer will it take for the cake to cool to 90°? (Round your answer to the nearest 5 minutes.)

   (A) 15 min   (B) 20 min   (C) 25 min
   (D) 30 min   (E) 35 min

2. _____

3.

Time (hours)	0	5	10	15	20
Population (thousands)	8	14	25	40	53

   The table shows the growth of a population of bacteria in a petri dish. Use logistic regression to determine the approximate carrying capacity (in thousands of bacteria).

   (A) 0.15   (B) 9.25   (C) 37.91 (D) 75.83 (E) 151.65

3. _____

4. The current population of Boomtown is $P(0) = 93{,}000$ and the relative growth rate is 8.7%. Assuming the growth rate remains constant, what will the population be after 7 years? (Round your answer to the nearest 5000.)

   (A) 165,000   (B) 170,000   (C) 175,000
   (D) 180,000   (E) 185,000

4. _____

5. Suppose the improved Euler's method is used to solve the initial value problem $y' = y^2 + \sin x$, $y(0) = -1$, starting at $x_0 = 0$ with $dx = 0.1$. What value is obtained for $y(2)$? (Round your answer to the nearest hundredth.)

   (A) 0.16   (B) 0.86   (C) 0.97   (D) 1.04   (E) 1.99

5. _____

6. Use Euler's method to solve the initial value problem graphically starting at $x_0 = 0$ with $dx = 0.1$. (Use a smooth curve to indicate the approximate solution.)
   $$y' = 0.2y - 0.2x, \quad y(0) = 1.5$$

6.

[0, 8] by [−3, 3]

Directions: Show all steps leading to your answers, including any intermediate results obtained using a graphing utility. Use the back of the test or another sheet of paper if necessary.

1. Use the Fundamental Theorem of Calculus to evaluate $\int e^{x^2 + \sin x}\, dx$.

1. _____

   (A) $\int_0^x (t^2 + \sin t)\, dt + C$ (B) $\int_x^0 e^{t^2 + \sin t}\, dt + C$

   (C) $\int_0^x (2t + \cos t)e^{t^2 + \sin t}\, dt + C$ (D) $\int_0^x e^{t^2 + \sin t}\, dt + C$

   (E) $(2x + \cos x)e^{x^2 + \sin x} + C$

2. Evaluate $\int (e^{3x} - 4 \cos x)\, dx$.

2. _____

3. Solve the initial value problem.
$$\frac{dy}{dx} = 5x^2 - 7,\ y(3) = 12$$

3. _____

4. Draw a possible graph for the function f with the given slope field that satisfies $y(0) = 1$.

4.

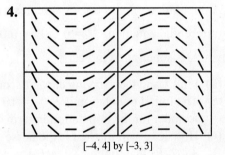

                      [–4, 4] by [–3, 3]

5. Use substitution to evaluate $\int \dfrac{(\ln x)^5\, dx}{x}$.

5. _____

6. Evaluate the definite integral by making a u-substitution and integrating from $u(a)$ to $u(b)$.
$$\int_0^{\pi/2} e^{\sin x} \cos x\, dx$$

6. _____

7. Use separation of variables to solve the initial value problem.
$$\frac{dy}{dx} = \frac{\cos x}{3y^2};\ y(\pi) = 5$$

7. _____

8. Use integration by parts to evaluate $\int \cos^{-1} 2x\, dx$.

8. _____

9. Evaluate $\int (4x^2 - 3x)e^x\, dx$.

9. _____

10. Evaluate $\int 2 \cos(\ln t)\, dt$ by using a substitution prior to integration by parts.

10. _____

11. The decay equation of a certain radioactive element is $y = y_0 e^{-1.2t}$, where t is measured in years. (Round answers to the nearest 0.001 year.)
    (a) What is the half-life of the element?
    (b) How many years will it take for 98% of a sample of this element to decay?

11. (a) _____
    (b) _____

12. A 1200-kg car coasts to a stop from a speed of 20 m/sec. The car's motion obeys the equation $v = v_0 e^{-(k/m)t}$ with $k = 80$ kg/sec.
    (a) About how far will the car coast before reaching a complete stop? (Round to the nearest whole meter.)
    (b) About how long will it take the car's speed to drop to 5 m/sec? (Round to the nearest 0.1 sec.)

12. (a) _____
    (b) _____

13. The relative growth rate of the population of Brockton is 0.031 and its current population is $P(0) = 56,800$.
    (a) Write a differential equation for the population.
    (b) Find a formula for the population P in terms of t.

13. (a) _____
    (b) _____

14. A population of wild horses is represented by the logistic differential equation $\dfrac{dP}{dt} = 0.08P - 0.00004P^2$, where t is measured in years.

    (a) Find k and the carrying capacity for the population.
    (b) The initial population is $P(0) = 10$ horses. Find a formula for the population in terms of t.
    (c) How long will it take for the horse population to reach 350? (Round to the nearest 0.1 year.)

14. (a) $k =$ _____

    carrying

    capacity = _____

    (b) _____
    (c) _____

15. Suppose Euler's method, with increment dx, is used to numerically solve the differential equation $\dfrac{dy}{dx} = f(x, y)$ with the initial condition that (x_0, y_0) lies on the solution curve. Let (x_1, y_1), (x_2, y_2), and so on denote the points generated by Euler's method, and let $y = y(x)$ denote the exact solution to the initial value problem. Which of the following must be true?
    I. $y_3 = y(x_3)$
    II. $y_2 = y_1 + f(x_1, y_1)\, dx$
    III. $x_3 = x_0 + 3\, dx$

    (A) II only   (B) I and II   (C) I and III
    (D) II and III   (E) I, II, and III

15. _____

16. Use the improved Euler's method to numerically solve the initial value problem $y' = e^x - 10y$, $y(2) = 3.5$, on the interval $2 \le x \le 3$ starting at $x_0 = 2$ with $dx = 0.1$. (Show y-values rounded to the nearest 0.001.)

16.

Directions: Show all steps leading to your answers, including any intermediate results obtained using a graphing utility. Use the back of the test or another sheet of paper if necessary.

1. Use the Fundamental Theorem of Calculus to evaluate
$\int \sin(e^x - 4x)\, dx$.

    1. _____

(A) $\int_0^x \sin(e^t - 4t)\, dt + C$ (B) $\int_x^0 (e^t - 4t)\, dt + C$

(C) $(e^x - 4)\cos(e^x - 4x) + C$ (D) $-\cos(e^x - 4x) + C$

(E) $\int_0^x (e^t - 4)\cos(e^t - 4t)\, dt + C$

2. Evaluate $\int (\cos 3x - 5e^x)\, dx$.

    2. _____

3. Solve the initial value problem.
$\dfrac{dy}{dx} = 8x^3 + 5,\ y(2) = 7$

    3. _____

4. Draw a possible graph for the function f with the given slope field that satisfies $y(0) = -1$.

    4.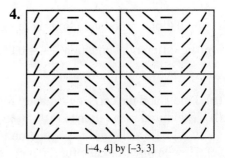

                       [−4, 4] by [−3, 3]

5. Use substitution to evaluate $\int (x^3 + x)e^{x^4 + 2x^2}\, dx$.

    5. _____

6. Evaluate the definite integral by making a u-substitution and integrating from $u(a)$ to $u(b)$.
$\int_1^e \dfrac{2\ln x - 6(\ln x)^2}{x}\, dx$

    6. _____

7. Use separation of variables to solve the initial value problem.
$\dfrac{dy}{dx} = 2x\cos^2 y;\ y(3) = 0$

    7. _____

8. Use integration by parts to evaluate $\int \cot^{-1} 3x\, dx$

    8. _____

9. Evaluate $\int e^{3x}\sin 2x\, dx$.

    9. _____

10. Evaluate $\int 2t^5 e^{t^2}\, dt$ by using a substitution prior to integration by parts.

    10. _____

11. The decay equation of a certain radioactive element is   11. (a) _____

    $y = y_0 e^{-1.6t}$, where t is measured in years. (Round   (b) _____

    answers to the nearest 0.001 year.)

    (a) What is the half-life of the element?
    (b) How many years will it take for 96% of a sample of
        this element to decay?

12. A 10,000-kg truck coasts to a stop from a speed of   12. (a) _____
    40 m/sec. The truck's motion obeys the equation   (b) _____
    $v = v_0 e^{-(k/m)t}$ with $k = 200$ kg/sec.
    (a) About how far will the truck coast before reaching a
        complete stop? (Round to the nearest whole meter.)
    (b) About how long will it take the truck's speed to drop
        to 7 m/sec? (Round to the nearest 0.1 sec.)

13. The relative growth rate of the population of Lynton is   13. (a) _____
    0.047 and its current population is $P(0) = 83,400$.   (b) _____
    (a) Write a differential equation for the population.
    (b) Find a formula for the population P in terms of t.

14. A population of mountain lions is represented by the   14. (a) $k = $ _____

    logistic differential equation $\dfrac{dP}{dt} = 0.06P - 0.000075P^2$,   carrying

    where t is measured in years.   capacity = _____

    (a) Find k and the carrying capacity for the population.   (b) _____
    (b) The initial population is $P(0) = 25$ mountain lions.   (c) _____
        Find a formula for the population in terms of t.
    (c) How long will it take for the mountain lion population
        to reach 450? (Round to the nearest 0.1 year.)

15. Suppose Euler's method, with increment dx, is used to   15. _____

    numerically solve the differential equation $\dfrac{dy}{dx} = f(x, y)$

    with the initial condition that (x_0, y_0) lies on the solution
    curve. Let (x_1, y_1), (x_2, y_2), and so on denote the points
    generated by Euler's method, and let $y = y(x)$ denote the
    exact solution to the initial value problem. Which of the
    following must be true?
    I. $x_2 = x_0 + 2\, dx$
    II. (x_1, y_1) lies (exactly) on the solution curve.
    III. $y_3 = y_2 + f(x_2, y_2)\, dx$

    (A) II only   (B) I and II   (C) I and III
    (D) II and III   (E) I, II, and III

16. Use the improved Euler's method to numerically solve   16.
    the initial value problem $y' = 4x - e^y$, $y(1) = 2.5$, on the
    interval $1 \le x \le 2$ starting at $x_0 = 1$ with $dx = 0.1$. (Show
    y-values rounded to the nearest 0.001.)

1. The function $v(t) = 12t^2 - 16t$ is the velocity in m/sec of a particle moving along the x-axis, where t is measured in seconds. Use analytic methods to find the particle's displacement for $0 \le t \le 5$. (Round to the nearest 10 m.)

   (A) 220 m (B) 260 m (C) 300 m (D) 310 m (E) 340 m

   1. _____

2. The graph of the velocity of a particle moving on the x-axis is given. The particle starts at $x = 4$ when $t = 0$. Find the particle's position at the end of the trip ($t = 5$).

   (A) $x = 3.5$ (B) $x = 4$ (C) $x = 4.5$
   (D) $x = 5.5$ (E) $x = 6.5$

   2. _____

   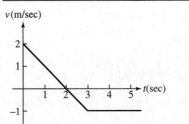

3. A certain spring obeys Hooke's Law and requires a force of 10 N to stretch it 8 cm beyond its natural length. How much work would be done in stretching the spring from its natural length to 12 cm beyond its natural length?

   (A) 15 N   (B) 25 N   (C) 60 N • cm
   (D) 90 N • cm   (E) 180 N • cm

   3. _____

4. Find the area of the shaded region. (Round to the nearest whole number.)

   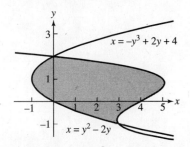

   (A) 10

   (B) 11

   (C) 12

   (D) 13

   (E) 14

   4. _____

5. Find the area of the region enclosed by $y = \sin 2x$ and $y = \cos x$ for $-\dfrac{\pi}{2} \le x \le \dfrac{\pi}{6}$.

   (A) 2.25   (B) 2.75   (C) 3   (D) $\dfrac{\pi}{2}$ (E) $\dfrac{3\pi}{4}$

   5. _____

6. The base of a solid is the region between the line $y = 4$ and the parabola $y = x^2$. The cross sections perpendicular to the x-axis are semicircles. Find the volume of the solid.

   (A) $\dfrac{16\pi}{3}$ (B) $\dfrac{64\pi}{3}$ (C) $\dfrac{64\pi}{15}$ (D) $\dfrac{128\pi}{15}$ (E) $\dfrac{512\pi}{15}$

   6. _____

7. A region is bounded by the lines $y = \sqrt{x}$, $y = x - 2$, and $y = 0$. Find the volume of the solid generated by rotating this region about the x-axis.

   (A) $\dfrac{8\pi}{3}$ (B) $\dfrac{16\pi}{3}$ (C) $\dfrac{20\pi}{3}$ (D) $\dfrac{24\pi}{3}$ (E) $\dfrac{32\pi}{3}$

   7. _____

1. Which of the following integrals gives the length of the curve $y = \sin 3x$ from $x = 0$ to $x = 5$?

1. _____

(A) $\int_0^5 \sqrt{1 + \sin^2 3x}\, dx$

(B) $\int_0^5 \sqrt{1 - 9 \sin 3x}\, dx$

(C) $\int_0^5 \sqrt{1 - 3 \cos 3x}\, dx$

(D) $\int_0^5 \sqrt{1 + 3 \cos 3x}\, dx$

(E) $\int_0^5 \sqrt{1 + 9 \cos^2 3x}\, dx$

2. Find the length of the curve $y = e^x - x^2$ from $x = -2$ to $x = 4$. (Round to the nearest multiple of 5.)

2. _____

(A) 25   (B) 30   (C) 35   (D) 40   (E) 45

3. Find the length of the curve $y = 2\sqrt[5]{x}$ from $x = -1$ to $x = 1$. (Round to the nearest half.)

3. _____

(A) 4.5   (B) 5   (C) 5.5   (D) 6   (E) 6.5

4. A chain weighs 0.5 pound per foot of length. If a 36-foot length of this chain is hanging from the edge of the roof of a tall building, how much work will it take to pull the chain up onto the roof? (Round to the nearest 25 ft-lb.)

4. _____

(A) 225 ft-lb   (B) 250 ft-lb   (C) 275 ft-lb
(D) 300 ft-lb   (E) 325 ft-lb

5. The mean weight of a certain brand of frozen dinner is 11.4 oz with a standard deviation of 0.3 oz. What percentage of the frozen dinners weigh between 11 and 12 oz? (Round to the nearest 5%.)

5. _____

(A) 75%   (B) 80%   (C) 85%   (D) 90%   (E) 95%

6. If a 2-kg object is dropped from rest, its kinetic energy E (in joules) increases according to the differential equation $\frac{dE}{dt} = 192t$, where t is measured in seconds. If the initial kinetic energy is 0J, what is the kinetic energy after 5 seconds?

6. _____

(A) 960 J   (B) 1440 J   (C) 1800 J
(D) 2400 J   (E) 4800 J

Directions: Show all steps leading to your answers, including any intermediate results obtained using a graphing utility. Use the back of the test or another sheet of paper if necessary.

1. The function $v(t) = t^2 - 4$ is the velocity in m/sec for a particle moving along the x-axis, where t is measured in seconds ($t \geq 0$). Use analytic methods to do each of the following:
   (a) Determine when the particle is moving to the right, to the left, and stopped.
   (b) Find the particle's displacement for $0 \leq t \leq 5$.
   (c) Find the total distance traveled by the particle for $0 \leq t \leq 5$.

   1. (a) Right: _____
          Left: _____
          Stopped: _____

   (b) _____
   (c) _____

2. The graph shows the velocity of a particle moving on the x-axis. The particle starts at $x = -3$ when $t = 0$.
   (a) Find where the particle is at the end of the trip ($t = 6$).
   (b) Find the total distance traveled by the particle.

   2. (a) _____
   (b) _____

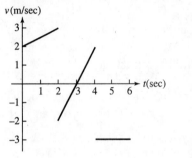

3. The rate of expenditures on public elementary and secondary schools (in billions of dollars per year) in the United States can be modeled by the function $S = 6.22e^{0.086t}$, where t is the number of years after January 1, 1950. Find the total expenditures from January 1, 1950 to January 1, 1990.

   3. _____

4. Find the area of the shaded region analytically.

   4. _____

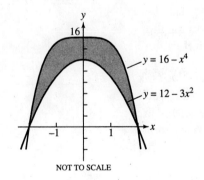

NOT TO SCALE

5. Find the area of the region enclosed by the line $y = 3x + 4$ and the parabola $y = x^2 - 3x - 12$.

   5. _____

6. Find the area enclosed by $y = \sqrt{x}$, $y = 6 - 2x$, and the x-axis.

   6. _____

   (A) 2.1468   (B) 2.7423   (C) 2.8125
   (D) 3.1036   (E) 3.6507

7. Find the volume generated by revolving the shaded region about the *x*-axis.

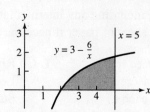

7. _____

8. A region is bounded by $y = \sqrt{16 + x^2}$ and $y = 5$ for $x \geq 0$. Use the cylindrical shell method to find the volume of the solid generated by revolving this region about the *y*-axis.

8. _____

9. Find the area of the surface generated by revolving the curve $y = \dfrac{x^3}{4}$, $0 < x < 1$, about the *x*-axis.

9. _____

10. A curve is given by $y = (9 - x^{2/3})^{3/2}$ for $1 \leq x \leq 8$. Find the exact length of the curve analytically by antidifferentiation.

10. _____

11. Find the length of the nonsmooth curve $y = x^{2/5}$ for $-1 \leq x \leq 1$. (Round your answer to the nearest 0.001.)

(A) 1.516 (B) 2.149 (C) 2.484
(D) 2.941 (E) 3.031

11. _____

12. A curve is given by $x = \displaystyle\int_0^y \sqrt{9t^2 + 6t}\, dt$ for $1 \leq y \leq 5$.

Find the exact length of the curve analytically by antidifferentiation.

12. _____

13. Suppose a spring has a natural length of 8 inches. To extend the spring 2 inches, a force of 3 pounds must be used. How much work would be required to stretch the spring from its natural length to twice its natural length?

13. _____

14. A right cylindrical tank is filled with sea water. The tank has a radius of 6 feet and a height of 12 feet. If the water level is now 3 feet below the top of the tank, how much work will be required to pump the sea water to the top of the tank? (The weight-density of seawater is 64 lb/ft^3.)

14. _____

15. For a certain species of fish, the mean length of an adult is 23.8 cm with a standard deviation of 4.2 cm.
(a) What percentage of the adult fish have a length of more than 28.0 cm?
(b) What percentage of the adult fish have a length between 20 cm and 26 cm?
(c) If we sample 350 adult fish at random, about how many should have a length of at least 22 cm?

15. (a) _____
(b) _____

Directions: Show all steps leading to your answers, including any intermediate results obtained using a graphing utility. Use the back of the test or another sheet of paper if necessary.

1. The function $v(t) = 9 - t^2$ is the velocity in m/sec for a particle moving along the x-axis, where t is measured in seconds ($t \geq 0$). Use analytic methods to do each of the following:
   (a) Determine when the particle is moving to the right, to the left, and stopped.
   (b) Find the particle's displacement for $0 \leq t \leq 6$.
   (c) Find the total distance traveled by the particle for $0 \leq t \leq 6$.

   1. (a) Right: _____
          Left: _____
          Stopped: _____

      (b) _____
      (c) _____

2. The graph shows the velocity of a particle moving on the x-axis. The particle starts at $x = -5$ when $t = 0$.
   (a) Find where the particle is at the end of the trip ($t = 6$).
   (b) Find the total distance traveled by the particle.

   2. (a) _____
      (b) _____

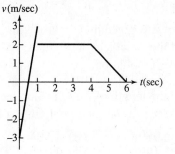

3. The rate of expenditures on public elementary and secondary schools (in billions of dollars per year) in the United States can be modeled by the function $A = 9.93e^{0.084t}$, where t is the number of years after January 1, 1960. Find the total expenditures from January 1, 1960 to January 1, 1990.

   3. _____

4. Find the area of the shaded region analytically.

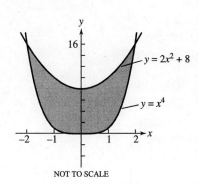

NOT TO SCALE

   4. _____

5. Find the area of the region enclosed by the line $y = 2x - 15$ and the parabola $y = -x^2 + 4x$.

   5. _____

6. Find the area enclosed by $y = 3\sqrt{x}$, $y = 20 - 2x$, and the x-axis.

   (A) 39.5736   (B) 45.3125   (C) 46.7382
   (D) 49.7318   (E) 54.1402

   6. _____

7. Find the volume generated by revolving the shaded region about the *x*-axis.

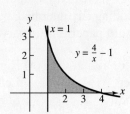

7. _____

8. A region is bounded by $y = \sqrt{25 - x^2}$ and $y = 3$ for $x \geq 0$. Use the cylindrical shell method to find the volume of the solid generated by revolving this region about the *y*-axis.

8. _____

9. Find the area of the surface generated by revolving the curve $y = \dfrac{x^3}{9}$, $0 < x < 2$, about the *x*-axis.

9. _____

10. A curve is given by $y = (16 - x^{2/3})^{3/2}$ for $1 \leq x \leq 27$. Find the exact length of the curve analytically by antidifferentiation.

10. _____

11. Find the length of the nonsmooth curve $y = x^{4/7}$ for $-1 \leq x \leq 1$. (Round your answer to the nearest 0.001.)

    (A) 2.919   (B) 2.894   (C) 2.410
    (D) 2.198   (E) 1.459

11. _____

12. A curve is given by $x = \displaystyle\int_0^y \sqrt{t^2 + 4t + 3}\, dt$ for $3 \leq y \leq 9$.

Find the exact length of the curve analytically by antidifferentiation.

12. _____

13. Suppose a spring has a natural length of 10 inches. To extend the spring 0.25 inches, a force of 25 pounds must be used. How much work would be required to stretch the spring from a length of 11 inches to a length of 12 inches?

13. _____

14. A right cylindrical tank is filled with sea water. The tank has a radius of 2 feet and a height of 8 feet. If the water level is now 2 feet below the top of the tank, how much work will be required to pump the sea water to the top of the tank? (The weight-density of seawater is 64 lb/ft³.)

14. _____

15. For a certain species of snake, the mean length of an adult is 63.4 cm with a standard deviation of 6.8 cm.
    (a) What percentage of the adult snakes have a length of more than 77.0 cm?
    (b) What percentage of the adult snakes have a length between 59 cm and 65 cm?
    (c) If we sample 450 adult snakes at random, about how many should have a length of at least 66 cm?

15. (a) _____
    (b) _____

1. Use l'Hôpital's rule to evaluate $\lim\limits_{x\to\pi} \dfrac{1 + \cos x}{\sin 2x}$.

  (A) -1 (B) $-\dfrac{1}{2}$ (C) 0 (D) $\dfrac{1}{2}$ (E) 1

1. _____

2. Use l'Hôpital's rule to evaluate $\lim\limits_{x\to 0} \dfrac{\sin 2x - 2\sin x}{\sin 3x - 3\sin x}$.

  (A) $-\dfrac{1}{2}$ (B) $-\dfrac{1}{4}$ (C) 0 (D) $\dfrac{1}{4}$ (E) $\dfrac{1}{2}$

2. _____

3. Use l'Hôpital's rule to evaluate $\lim\limits_{x\to\infty} \dfrac{\tan\dfrac{1}{x}}{\ln\left(1 + \dfrac{4}{x}\right)}$.

  (A) $-\dfrac{1}{4}$ (B) 0 (C) $\dfrac{1}{4}$ (D) 1 (E) ∞

3. _____

4. Use l'Hôpital's rule to evaluate $\lim\limits_{x\to\infty}\left(1 + \dfrac{1}{x^2}\right)^x$

  (A) 0 (B) 1 (C) e^{-2} (D) e^{-4} (E) ∞

4. _____

5. Which grows faster as $x \to \infty$, $\ln x$ or x^3?

  (A) $\ln x$ grows faster.   (B) x^3 grows faster.
  (C) They grow at the same rate.

5. _____

6. Which grows faster as $x \to \infty$, $(x-4)^3$ or $2x^3 + \ln x$?

  (A) $(x-4)^3$ grows faster   (B) $2x^3 + \ln x$ grows faster.
  (C) They grow at the same rate.

6. _____

7. Let $f(x) = x^5 + \cos x$ and $g(x) = e^x - x^3$ which of the
following are true?
  I. $f = o(g)$ II. $f = O(g)$
 III. $g = o(f)$ IV. $g = O(f)$
  (A) I only   (B) I and II   (C) II only
  (D) III only   (E) III and IV

7. _____

8. Use the graph of $y = \dfrac{f(x)}{g(x)}$ to determine which one of
the following is true.

8. _____

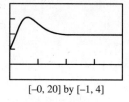

[–0, 20] by [–1, 4]

  (A) $f = o(g)$ (B) $g = o(f)$

  (C) f and g grow at the same rate.

1. Which one of the following integrals converges?

1. _____

   (A) $\int_0^4 \dfrac{\ln x}{x}\, dx$ (B) $\int_0^{\pi/2} \tan x\, dx$ (C) $\int_0^5 \dfrac{dx}{x + x^2}$

   (D) $\int_0^9 \dfrac{dx}{\sqrt{9 - x}}$ (E) $\int_0^3 \dfrac{dx}{x^2}$

2. Which one of the following integrals diverges?

2. _____

   (A) $\int_1^{\infty} \dfrac{dx}{\sqrt{x} + \ln x}$ (B) $\int_1^{\infty} \dfrac{dx}{x^2 + 5}$ (C) $\int_1^{\infty} e^{-x^2}\, dx$

   (D) $\int_1^{\infty} e^{-x}\, dx$ (E) $\int_1^{\infty} \dfrac{3 - 2\sin x}{x^2}\, dx$

3. Evaluate the integral $\int_0^1 x \ln x\, dx$ or state that it diverges.

3. _____

   (A) -1 (B) $-\dfrac{1}{4}$ (C) $\dfrac{1}{4}$ (D) $\dfrac{1}{2}$

   (E) It diverges.

4. Evaluate the integral $\int_2^{\infty} \dfrac{x\, dx}{(x^2 - 1)^2}$ or state that it diverges.

4. _____

   (A) $-\dfrac{1}{3}$ (B) $-\dfrac{1}{6}$ (C) $\dfrac{1}{6}$ (D) $\dfrac{1}{3}$

   (E) It diverges.

5. Use partial fractions to evaluate $\int \dfrac{20x + 16}{x^2 + 3x + 2}\, dx$.

5. _____

   (A) $3 \ln |x + 2| - \ln |x + 1| + C$

   (B) $3 \ln |x + 2| + 2 \ln |x + 1| + C$

   (C) $2 \ln |x + 2| - 3 \ln |x + 1| + C$

   (D) $24 \ln |x + 2| - 4 \ln |x + 1| + C$

   (E) $20 \ln |x + 2| + 16 \ln |x + 1| + C$

6. Use analytic methods to find the volume of the solid generated by revolving the shaded region about the x-axis.

6. _____

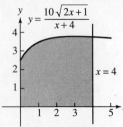

   (A) $(100 \ln 2 - 75)\pi$

   (B) $100(\ln 8 - 1)\pi$

   (C) 50π

   (D) $(200 \ln 2 - 87.5)\pi$

   (E) The volume cannot be determined because the integral diverges.

7. Which trigonometric substitution would be most useful in evaluating $\int (25 + x^2)\, dx$?

7. _____

   (A) $x = 5 \tan \theta$ (B) $x = 5 \sin \theta$ (C) $x = 5 \sec \theta$

   (D) $x = 25 \tan \theta$ (E) $x = 25 \sec \theta$

Directions: Show all steps leading to your answers, including any intermediate results obtained using a graphing utility. Use the back of the test or another sheet of paper if necessary.

1. Use l'Hôpital's rule to evaluate $\lim\limits_{x \to 2} \dfrac{x^3 - 2x^2 + x - 2}{x^2 + x - 6}$.
Support your answer graphically.

1. _____

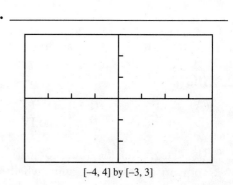

$[-4, 4]$ by $[-3, 3]$

2. Let $f(x) = \dfrac{7x^2 - 8x + 3}{4x^2 + 5}$.

   (a) Complete the table and estimate $\lim\limits_{x \to \infty} f(x)$.

   (b) Use l'Hôpital's rule to confirm your estimate.

2. (a)

x	$f(x)$
10	
10^2	
10^3	
10^4	
10^5	

Limit _____

   (b) _____

_____

3. Use l'Hôpital's rule to find the exact value of
$\lim\limits_{x \to 0} (e^{5/x} - 3x)^{x/2}$.

3. _____

4. A student attempted to use l'Hôpital's rule as follows. Identify the student's error, if any, or state "No error."

$$\lim_{x \to \infty} \frac{\sin (1/x)}{e^{1/x}} = \lim_{x \to \infty} \frac{-x^{-2} \cos (1/x)}{-x^{-2} e^{1/x}}$$

$$= \lim_{x \to \infty} \frac{\cos 1/x}{e^{1/x}} = \frac{1}{1} = 1$$

4. _____

5. Determine which function grows faster as $x \to \infty$, $\ln (x^2 + 4)$ or $x - 5$.

   (A) $\ln (x^2 + 4)$ grows faster. (B) $x - 5$ grows faster.

   (C) They grow at the same rate.

5. _____

6. Order the functions e^{2x}, x^6, $3x^5$, and $(\ln x)^2$ from slowest-growing to fastest-growing as $x \to \infty$.

6. _____

7. Show that the functions $f_1(x) = 5^x$, $f_2(x) = 5^{x-3}$, and $f_3(x) = 5^x + 3^x$ all grow at the same rate as $x \to \infty$.

7. _____

8. Let $f(x) = x^3 - 4x^2$ and $g(x) = 5x^3 + 2x$.
Which of the following are true?
 I. $f = o(g)$ II. $f = O(g)$
 III. $g = o(f)$ IV. $g = O(f)$

 (A) I only   (B) I and II   (C) III only
 (D) III and IV   (E) II and IV

8. _____

9. Use integration, the direct comparison test, or the limit comparison test to determine whether each integral converges or diverges.

 (a) $\displaystyle\int_0^2 \frac{dx}{4 - x^2}$

 (b) $\displaystyle\int_0^\infty (5 + \cos x)e^{-x}\, dx$

 (c) $\displaystyle\int_0^\infty x^{-3}\, dx$

9. (a) _____
   (b) _____
   (c) _____

10. Evaluate $\displaystyle\int_0^3 \frac{x}{\sqrt{9 - x^2}}\, dx$ or state that it diverges.

10. _____

11. Evaluate $\displaystyle\int_e^\infty \frac{3\, dx}{x(\ln x)^2}$ or state that it diverges.

11. _____

12. Find the area of the region in the first quadrant that lies under the graph of $y = (3x^2 + x)e^{-x}$.

12. _____

13. Express $\dfrac{-2x^2 + 10x + 8}{x^2(x + 2)}$ as a sum of partial fractions.

13. _____

14. Use partial fractions to evaluate $\displaystyle\int \frac{4x + 30}{x^2 + x - 12}\, dx$.

14. _____

15. Solve the initial value problem.
 $\dfrac{dy}{dx} = (y^2 - 2y)\cos x, \; y(1) = 1.$

15. _____

16. Use a trigonometric substitution to evaluate $\displaystyle\int x^3\sqrt{36 - x^2}\, dx$.

16. _____

Directions: Show all steps leading to your answers, including any intermediate results obtained using a graphing utility. Use the back of the test or another sheet of paper if necessary.

1. Use l'Hôpital's rule to evaluate $\lim\limits_{x\to 1} \dfrac{x^2 + 4x - 5}{x^3 - 5x^2 + 4x}$.
Support your answer graphically.

1. _____

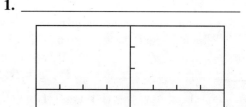

[-4, 4] by [-3, 3]

2. Let $f(x) = \dfrac{5x^2 - 6}{3x^2 - 5x + 8}$.

  (a) Complete the table and estimate $\lim\limits_{x\to\infty} f(x)$.

  (b) Use l'Hôpital's rule to confirm your estimate.

2. **(a)**

x	$f(x)$
10	
10^2	
10^3	
10^4	
10^5	

Limit _____

  (b) _____

_____

3. Use l'Hôpital's rule to find the exact value of
$\lim\limits_{x\to\infty} (e^{3x} + 5x)^{2/x}$.

3. _____

4. A student attempted to use l'Hôpital's rule as follows. Identify the student's error, if any, or state "No error."

$$\lim_{x\to 0} \frac{4x^2 - 5x + 1}{2x^2 + 3x - 5} = \lim_{x\to 0} \frac{8x - 5}{4x + 3}$$

$$= \lim_{x\to 0} \frac{8}{4} = 2$$

4. _____

5. Determine which function grows faster as $x \to \infty$, $e^{\sqrt{x/2}}$ or $x^5 + 2$.

  (A) $e^{\sqrt{x/2}}$ grows faster.   (B) $x^5 + 2$ grows faster.

  (C) They grow at the same rate.

5. _____

6. Order the functions $4x^2$, $(\ln x)^3$, 10^x, and e^{2x} from slowest-growing to fastest-growing as $x \to \infty$.

6. _____

7. Show that the functions $f_1(x) = x^5$, $f_2(x) = 2x^5 + x^2$, and $f_3(x) = x^5 + \ln x$ all grow at the same rate as $x \to \infty$.

7. _____
   _____
   _____

8. Let $f(x) = 6x^2 + 7x$ and $g(x) = x^3 - 4x^2$.
Which of the following are true?
I. $f = o(g)$ II. $f = O(g)$
III. $g = o(f)$ IV. $g = O(f)$

(A) I only   (B) I and II   (C) III only
(D) III and IV   (E) II and IV

8. _____

9. Use integration, the direct comparison test, or the limit comparison test to determine whether each integral converges or diverges.

9. (a) _____
   (b) _____
   (c) _____

(a) $\displaystyle\int_0^\infty x^{-0.5}\, dx$

(b) $\displaystyle\int_3^4 \frac{dx}{x^2 - 9}$

(c) $\displaystyle\int_1^\infty (3 + 2\cos x)x^{-4}\, dx$

10. Evaluate $\displaystyle\int_{e^2}^\infty \frac{2\, dx}{x(\ln x)^3}$ or state that it diverges.

10. _____

11. Evaluate $\displaystyle\int_0^{\pi/4} \frac{\cos 2x}{\sqrt{\sin 2x}}\, dx$ or state that it diverges.

11. _____

12. Find the area of the region in the first quadrant that lies under the graph of $y = (x^2 + 2x)e^{-x}$.

12. _____

13. Express $\dfrac{7x^2 - 16x + 5}{x(x-1)^2}$ as a sum of partial fractions.

13. _____

14. Use partial fractions to evaluate $\displaystyle\int \frac{x - 13}{x^2 + 4x - 5}\, dx$.

14. _____

15. Solve the initial value problem.
$$\frac{dy}{dx} = \frac{\csc y}{x^2 + 3x}, \quad y(1) = \frac{\pi}{2}.$$

15. _____

16. Use a trigonometric substitution to evaluate
$$\int \frac{x^3\, dx}{(49 - x^2)^{3/2}}.$$

16. _____

For questions 1–4, refer to the following choices. (Any of these choices may be used more than once.)

(A) $1 - \dfrac{2}{3} + \dfrac{4}{9} - \dfrac{8}{27} + \cdots$ (B) $3 + 2 + \dfrac{4}{3} + \dfrac{8}{9} + \cdots$ (C) $\dfrac{1}{2} + \dfrac{2}{3} + \dfrac{3}{4} + \dfrac{4}{5} + \cdots$

(D) $\dfrac{256}{243} + \dfrac{128}{81} + \dfrac{64}{27} + \dfrac{32}{9} + \cdots$ (E) $\dfrac{3}{4} - \dfrac{9}{16} + \dfrac{27}{64} - \dfrac{81}{256} + \cdots$

1. Which series above converges to $\dfrac{3}{5}$?

1. _____

2. Which series above is a divergent geometric series?

2. _____

3. Which series above is *not* geometric?

3. _____

4. Which series above can be represented as $\displaystyle\sum_{n=0}^{\infty} \left(-\dfrac{2}{3}\right)^n$?

4. _____

For questions 5–7, refer to the following choices. (Any of these choices may be used more than once.)

(A) $-1 + x + x^2 + x^3 + \cdots + x^n + \cdots$ (B) $x + \dfrac{x^2}{2} + \dfrac{x^3}{3} + \dfrac{x^4}{4} + \cdots + \dfrac{x^n}{n} + \cdots$

(C) $1 + x + \dfrac{x^2}{2} + \dfrac{x^3}{6} + \cdots + \dfrac{x^n}{n!} + \cdots$ (D) $x + x^2 + \dfrac{x^3}{2} + \dfrac{x^4}{6} + \cdots + \dfrac{x^n}{(n-1)!} + \cdots$

(E) $x + 2x^2 + 3x^3 + 4x^4 + \cdots + nx^n + \cdots$

5. Which series above is the Maclaurin series for e^x?

5. _____

6. Let $f(x)$ be a continuous function whose third order Taylor polynomial at $x = 0$ is $1 + \dfrac{x^2}{2} + \dfrac{x^3}{6}$. Which series above could be the Taylor series at $x = 0$ for $f'(x)$?

6. _____

7. Let $g(x)$ be a continuous function with $g'''(0) = 3$. Which series above could be the Maclaurin series for $g(x)$?

7. _____

8. Use a graphical method to determine the approximate interval for which the second order Taylor polynomial for $\ln(1 + x)$ at $x = 0$ approximates $\ln(1 + x)$ with an absolute error of no more than 0.04.

8. _____

(A) $-0.1928 \le x \le 0.2062$ (B) $-0.4310 \le x \le 0.5525$

(C) $-0.3394 \le x \le 0.2640$ (D) $-0.5525 \le x \le 0.5525$

(E) $-0.5450 \le x \le 0.7063$

9. The polynomial $1 - x + x^2$ is used to estimate $\dfrac{1}{1 + x}$ on the interval $-0.15 \le x \le 0.15$. Use the Remainder Estimation Theorem to estimate the maximum possible error. (Round your answer to the nearest 0.0005.)

9. _____

(A) 0.0010   (B) 0.0020   (C) 0.0040
(D) 0.0065   (E) 0.0085

1. Which one of the following series diverges?

1. _____

(A) $\displaystyle\sum_{n=1}^{\infty} \frac{1}{n\sqrt{n}}$ (B) $\displaystyle\sum_{n=1}^{\infty} \left(-\frac{2}{3}\right)^n$ (C) $\displaystyle\sum_{n=2}^{\infty} \frac{1}{\ln n}$

(D) $\displaystyle\sum_{n=1}^{\infty} \frac{2^n}{n!}$ (E) $\displaystyle\sum_{n=1}^{\infty} \frac{\cos n}{n^2}$

2. Find the radius of convergence for $\displaystyle\sum_{n=0}^{\infty} \frac{(2x-5)^n}{n!}$

2. _____

(A) 0   (B) $\frac{1}{2}$ (C) 1   (D) 2   (E) ∞

3. Find the interval of convergence for $\displaystyle\sum_{n=0}^{\infty} \frac{(x^3-2)^{2n}}{4^n}$.

3. _____

(A) $-\sqrt[3]{4} < x < \sqrt[3]{4}$ (B) $-\sqrt[3]{2} < x < \sqrt[3]{6}$

(C) $0 < x < \sqrt[3]{4}$ (D) $0 \le x < \sqrt[3]{4}$

(E) $0 < x \le \sqrt[3]{4}$

4. The series $\displaystyle\sum_{n=0}^{\infty} \frac{(x^3-2)^{2n}}{4^n}$ sums to what function on its interval of convergence?

4. _____

(A) $\dfrac{x^6-4x^3+4}{4x^3-x^6}$ (B) $\dfrac{4}{x^6-4x^3+8}$ (C) $\dfrac{x^6-4x^3-4}{x^6-4x^3}$

(D) $\dfrac{4}{6-x^3}$ (E) $\dfrac{4}{4x^3-x^6}$

5. Describe the convergence or divergence of $\displaystyle\sum_{n=1}^{\infty} \frac{(-1)^n(2n-1)!}{n^5}$

5. _____

(A) Converges absolutely   (B) Converges conditionally
(C) Diverges

6. Describe the convergence or divergence of $\displaystyle\sum_{n=1}^{\infty} \frac{(-1)^n}{n}$

6. _____

(A) Converges absolutely   (B) Converges conditionally
(C) Diverges

7. For which series is the interval of convergence $(-2, 2]$?

7. _____

(A) $\displaystyle\sum_{n=1}^{\infty} \frac{(-2x)^n}{n}$ (B) $\displaystyle\sum_{n=1}^{\infty} \frac{(2x)^n}{n}$ (C) $\displaystyle\sum_{n=1}^{\infty} \frac{(-1)^n x^n}{n \cdot 2^n}$

(D) $\displaystyle\sum_{n=1}^{\infty} \frac{x^n}{n \cdot 2^n}$ (E) $\displaystyle\sum_{n=1}^{\infty} \left(-\frac{x}{2}\right)^n$

            © Addison Wesley Longman, Inc.

Directions: Show all steps leading to your answers, including any intermediate results obtained using a graphing utility. Use the back of the test or another sheet of paper if necessary.

1. Write the first four terms of the series $\sum_{n=2}^{\infty} \frac{x^n}{3n-1}$.

1. _____

2. Tell whether the series $\sum_{n=1}^{\infty} 4\left(\frac{2}{5}\right)^n$ converges or diverges. If it converges, find its sum.

2. _____

3. Express the repeating decimal $0.\overline{621}$ as a geometric series and find its sum.

3. _____

4. Given that $1 - x + x^2 + \cdots + (-x)^n$ is a power series representation for $\frac{1}{1+x}$, find a power series representation for $\frac{x^3}{1+x^2}$.

4. _____

5. Find the Taylor polynomial of order 3 generated by $f(x) = \sin 2x$ at $x = \frac{\pi}{4}$.

5. _____

6. Let f be a function that has derivatives of all orders for all real numbers. Assume $f(0) = 5, f'(0) = -3$, $f''(0) = 8$, and $f'''(0) = 24$. Write the third order Taylor polynomial for f at $x = 0$ and use it to approximate $f(0.4)$.

6. $P_3(x) =$ _____
$f(0.4) \approx$ _____

7. The Maclaurin series for $f(x)$ is
$1 + 2x + \frac{3x^2}{2} + \frac{4x^3}{6} + \cdots + \frac{(n+1)x^n}{n!} + \cdots$.
   (a) Find $f''(0)$.
   (b) Let $g(x) = x f'(x)$. Write the Maclaurin series for $g(x)$.
   (c) Let $h(x) = \int_0^x f(t)\, dt$. Write the Maclaurin series for $h(x)$.

7. (a) _____
   (b) _____
   (c) _____

8. Find the Taylor polynomial of order 4 for $f(x) = \ln(1 - x^2)$ at $x = 0$ and use it to approximate $f(0.3)$.

8. $P_4(x) =$ _____
$f(0.3) \approx$ _____

9. The polynomial $1 + 7x + 21x^2$ is used to approximate $f(x) = (1+x)^7$ on the interval $-0.01 \le x \le 0.01$.
   (a) Use the Remainder Estimation Theorem to estimate the maximum absolute error.
   (b) Use a graphical method to find the actual maximum absolute error.

9. (a) _____
   (b) _____

10. Use Euler's formula to write $\dfrac{e^{3i\theta} - e^{-3i\theta}}{i}$ as a trigonometric function of θ.

10. _____

    (A) $\sin 3\theta$ (B) $\cos 3\theta$ (C) $2\sin 3\theta$
    (D) $2\cos 3\theta$ (E) $-\sin 3\theta$

11. Determine the convergence or divergence of each series. Identify the test (or tests) you use.

11. (a) _____

    (b) _____

    (a) $\displaystyle\sum_{n=2}^{\infty} \dfrac{(2n)!}{(n-1)3^n}$ (b) $\displaystyle\sum_{n=1}^{\infty} \dfrac{(n^2 + 3n - 4)}{n!}$

    (c) _____

    (c) $\displaystyle\sum_{n=1}^{\infty} \left(1 + \dfrac{1}{2n}\right)^{3n}$

12. Determine whether each series converges absolutely, converges conditionally, or diverges.

12. (a) _____

    (b) _____

    (a) $\displaystyle\sum_{n=1}^{\infty} \dfrac{(-1)^n}{n^3 - \ln n}$ (b) $\displaystyle\sum_{n=1}^{\infty} \dfrac{\cos n\pi}{n^{2/3}}$

    (c) _____

    (c) $\displaystyle\sum_{n=1}^{\infty} \dfrac{(-1)^n n^3}{2^{n+2}}$

13. Find the radius of convergence of each power series.

13. (a) _____

    (a) $\displaystyle\sum_{n=0}^{\infty} \dfrac{(5x)^n}{3^n}$ (b) $\displaystyle\sum_{n=1}^{\infty} \dfrac{n^2(2x - 3)^n}{6^n}$

    (b) _____

14. Find the interval of convergence of the series $\displaystyle\sum_{n=0}^{\infty} \dfrac{(4x - 3)^{3n}}{8^n}$ and, within this interval, the sum of the series as a function of x.

14. Interval: _____

    Sum: _____

15. Determine all values of x for which the series $\displaystyle\sum_{n=1}^{\infty} \dfrac{2^n \sin^n x}{n^2}$ converges.

15. _____

16. Find the interval of convergence of the series $\displaystyle\sum_{n=1}^{\infty} \dfrac{3^n(x - 2)^n}{\sqrt{n + 2} \cdot 2^n}$.

16. _____

17. Suppose the interval of convergence of the Maclaurin series for $f(x)$ is $-2 < x < 2$. If the Maclaurin series for $\displaystyle\int_0^x f(t)\, dt$ is obtained by integrating term-by-term, which of the following could be the interval of convergence of new series?

17. _____

    I. $-2 < x < 2$ II. $-2 \le x < 2$
    III. $-2 < x \le 2$ IV. $-2 \le x \le 2$

    (A) I only   (B) I, II, or III   (C) II or III
    (D) IV only   (E) I, II, III, or IV

Directions: Show all steps leading to your answers, including any intermediate results obtained using a graphing utility. Use the back of the test or another sheet of paper if necessary.

1. Write the first four terms of the series $\sum_{n=3}^{\infty} \dfrac{x^n}{2n-1}$.

1. _____

2. Tell whether the series $\sum_{n=1}^{\infty} 5\left(\dfrac{3}{4}\right)^n$ converges or diverges. If it converges, find its sum.

2. _____

3. Express the repeating decimal $0.\overline{516}$ as a geometric series and find its sum.

3. _____

4. Given that $x - \dfrac{x^2}{2} + \dfrac{x^3}{3} + \cdots + \dfrac{(-1)^{n-1}x^n}{n}$ is a power series representation for $\ln(1+x)$, find a power series representation for $x^2 \ln(1+x^3)$.

4. _____

5. Find the Taylor polynomial of order 3 generated by $f(x) = \cos 3x$ at $x = \dfrac{\pi}{3}$.

5. _____

6. Let f be a function that has derivatives of all orders for all real numbers. Assume $f(0) = 9, f'(0) = 5$, $f''(0) = -4$, and $f'''(0) = 36$. Write the third order Taylor polynomial for f at $x = 0$ and use it to approximate $f(0.3)$.

6. $P_3(x) =$ _____
   $f(0.3) \approx$ _____

7. The Maclaurin series for $f(x)$ is
   $2x + 3x^2 + \dfrac{4x^3}{2} + \dfrac{5x^4}{6} + \cdots + \dfrac{(n+1)x^n}{(n-1)!} + \cdots$.
   (a) Find $f''(0)$.
   (b) Let $g(x) = x f'(x)$. Write the Maclaurin series for $g(x)$.
   (c) Let $h(x) = \int_0^x f(t)\, dt$. Write the Maclaurin series for $h(x)$.

7. (a) _____
   (b) _____
   (c) _____

8. Find the Taylor polynomial of order 4 for $f(x) = \dfrac{1}{1+x^2}$ at $x = 0$ and use it to approximate $f(0.2)$.

8. $P_4(x) =$ _____
   $f(0.2) \approx$ _____

9. The polynomial $1 + 6x + 15x^2$ is used to approximate $f(x) = (1+x)^6$ on the interval $-0.02 \le x \le 0.02$.

   (a) Use the Remainder Estimation Theorem to estimate the maximum absolute error.

   (b) Use a graphical method to find the actual maximum absolute error.

9. (a) _____
   (b) _____

10. Use Euler's formula to write $e^{4i\theta} + e^{-4i\theta}$ as a trigonometric function of θ.

    (A) $\sin 4\theta$ (B) $\cos 4\theta$ (C) $2 \sin 4\theta$

    (D) $2 \cos 4\theta$ (E) $-\sin 4\theta$

10. _____

11. Determine the convergence or divergence of each series. Identify the test (or tests) you use.

    (a) $\displaystyle\sum_{n=1}^{\infty} \frac{n^3}{(2n-1)!}$ (b) $\displaystyle\sum_{n=1}^{\infty} \left(1 + \frac{1}{5n}\right)^{2n}$

    (c) $\displaystyle\sum_{n=1}^{\infty} \frac{1}{n^2 + \sqrt{n}}$

11. (a) _____
   (b) _____
   (c) _____

12. Determine whether each series converges absolutely, converges conditionally, or diverges.

    (a) $\displaystyle\sum_{n=1}^{\infty} \frac{(-1)^n(n-1)^3}{(n+1)^3}$ (b) $\displaystyle\sum_{n=1}^{\infty} \frac{(-1)^n n^4}{3^{n-1}}$

    (c) $\displaystyle\sum_{n=1}^{\infty} \frac{\cos n\pi}{n^{4/3}}$

12. (a) _____
   (b) _____
   (c) _____

13. Find the radius of convergence of each power series.

    (a) $\displaystyle\sum_{n=0}^{\infty} \frac{(4x)^n}{7^n}$ (b) $\displaystyle\sum_{n=1}^{\infty} \frac{(3x-4)^n}{n \cdot 5^n}$

13. (a) _____
   (b) _____

14. Find the interval of convergence of the series $\displaystyle\sum_{n=0}^{\infty} \frac{(4x-5)^{2n}}{9^n}$ and, within this interval, the sum of the series as a function of x.

14. Interval: _____
   Sum: _____

15. Determine all values of x for which the series $\displaystyle\sum_{n=1}^{\infty} \frac{n}{2^n \cos^n x}$ converges.

15. _____

16. Find the interval of convergence of the series $\displaystyle\sum_{n=0}^{\infty} \frac{(-2)^n(x+1)^n}{(n+2)3^n}$.

16. _____

17. Suppose the interval of convergence of the Maclaurin series for $f(x)$ is $-3 \leq x < 3$. If the Maclaurin series for $f(-x)$ is obtained by replacing x by $-x$, which of the following could be the interval of convergence of new series?

    I. $-3 < x < 3$ II. $-3 \leq x < 3$

    III. $-3 < x \leq 3$ IV. $-3 \leq x \leq 3$

    (A) I only   (B) II only   (C) III only

    (D) II or III   (E) II, III, or IV

17. _____

1. Let $x = \sin 4t$ and $y = \cos 4t$. Find $\dfrac{d^2y}{dx^2}$ in terms of t.

1. _____

   (A) $-\tan 4t$ (B) $\cot^3 4t$ (C) $-16\tan 4t$
   (D) $-\sec^3 4t$ (E) -4

2. Find the length of the curve parametrized by $x = 3t$,
$y = \dfrac{1}{3}t^{3/2}$, $0 \le t \le 28$. Round your answer to the nearest
multiple of 10.

2. _____

   (A) 90   (B) 100   (C) 110   (D) 120   (E) 130

3. Let $\mathbf{u} = \langle -2, 1 \rangle$ and $\mathbf{v} = \langle 3, -1 \rangle$. Find the magnitude of
$3\mathbf{u} - 2\mathbf{v}$. (Round your answer to the nearest integer, if
necessary.)

3. _____

   (A) 2   (B) 8   (C) 10   (D) 12   (E) 13

4. Which of the following is a unit vector tangent to the
curve parametrized by $x = -2t^2 - 8t + 14$, $y = t^3$,
at $t = 2$?

4. _____

   (A) $\left\langle \dfrac{4}{5}, -\dfrac{3}{5} \right\rangle$ (B) $\left\langle \dfrac{4}{5}, \dfrac{3}{5} \right\rangle$ (C) $\left\langle \dfrac{3}{5}, -\dfrac{4}{5} \right\rangle$

   (D) $\left\langle \dfrac{3}{5}, \dfrac{4}{5} \right\rangle$ (E) $\langle -4, 3 \rangle$

5. The position vector of a particle in the plane is given by
$\mathbf{r}(t) = (t^2 - 3)\mathbf{i} + \left(\dfrac{t^3}{3} \right)\mathbf{j}$ for $-2 \le t \le 2$. Draw a graph of
the path of the particle.

5.

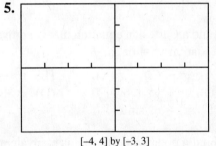

[-4, 4] by [-3, 3]

6. Find the velocity vector of the particle in question 5.

6. _____

   (A) $(2t)\mathbf{i} - (t^2)\mathbf{j}$ (B) $(2t)\mathbf{i} + (t^2)\mathbf{j}$
   (C) $2\mathbf{i} + (2t)\mathbf{j}$ (D) $(t^2)\mathbf{i} - (2t)\mathbf{j}$
   (E) $\left(\dfrac{t^3}{3} \right)\mathbf{i} - (t^2 - 3)\mathbf{j}$

7. Solve the initial value problem for $\mathbf{r}$ as a function of t.

7. _____

   $\dfrac{d\mathbf{r}}{dt} = (\cos t)\mathbf{i} + (4t^3 + 5)\mathbf{j}$, $\mathbf{r}(0) = -5\mathbf{j}$

   (A) $(\sin t)\mathbf{i} + (t^4)\mathbf{j}$ (B) $(\sin t)\mathbf{i} + (t^4 - 5)\mathbf{j}$
   (C) $(\sin t)\mathbf{i} + (t^4 + 5t - 5)\mathbf{j}$ (D) $(-\sin t)\mathbf{i} + (12t^2 - 5)\mathbf{j}$
   (E) $(-\cos t)\mathbf{i} + \left(\dfrac{1}{5}t^5 + \dfrac{5}{2}t^2 - 5 \right)\mathbf{j}$

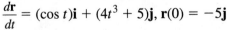

1. An ideal projectile is launched from the origin at an angle
   of α radians to the horizontal and an initial speed of
   100 ft/sec. Find the position function $\mathbf{r}(t)$ for this projectile.

   1. _____

   (A) $\mathbf{r}(t) = (100t \cos \alpha - 32\,t^2)\mathbf{i} + (100t \sin \alpha)\mathbf{j}$

   (B) $\mathbf{r}(t) = (100t \sin \alpha)\mathbf{i} + (100t \cos \alpha - 16t^2)\mathbf{j}$

   (C) $\mathbf{r}(t) = (100t \sin \alpha - 16t^2)\mathbf{i} + (100t \cos \alpha)\mathbf{j}$

   (D) $\mathbf{r}(t) = (100t \cos \alpha)\mathbf{i} + (100t \sin \alpha - 16t^2)\mathbf{j}$

   (E) $\mathbf{r}(t) = (100t \cos \alpha)\mathbf{i} + (100t \sin \alpha - 32t^2)\mathbf{j}$

2. An ideal projectile is launched from level ground at a
   launch angle of 26° and an initial speed of 48 m/sec. How
   far away from the launch point does the projectile hit the
   ground?

   2. _____

   (A) ≈60 m   (B) ≈185 m   (C) ≈230 m
   (D) ≈290 m   (E) ≈370 m

3. Graph the polar curve given by $r = 1.5 + 1.5 \sin \theta$.

   3.
   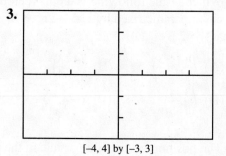
   [–4, 4] by [–3, 3]

4. Find a Cartesian equation that is equivalent to the polar
   equation $r^2 = 6r \sin \theta$.

   4. _____

   (A) $x^2 + 6x + y^2 = 0$ (B) $x^2 - 6x + y^2 = 0$
   (C) $x^2 + y^2 + 6y = 0$ (D) $x^2 + y^2 - 6y = 0$
   (E) $y^2 = 6y \sin x$

5. Find a polar equation that is equivalent to the Cartesian
   equation $y = 2x^2$.

   5. _____

   (A) $r = \dfrac{1}{2} \tan \theta$ (B) $r = \dfrac{1}{2} \sec^2 \theta$ (C) $r = \dfrac{2 \sin \theta}{\cos^2 \theta}$

   (D) $r = \dfrac{\cos \theta}{2 \sin^2 \theta}$ (E) $r = \dfrac{\sin \theta}{2 \cos^2 \theta}$

6. Find the slope of the polar curve $r = 3 + 4 \cos \theta$ at $\theta = \dfrac{\pi}{2}$.

   6. _____

   (A) $-\dfrac{3}{4}$ (B) $\dfrac{3}{4}$ (C) $-\dfrac{4}{3}$ (D) $\dfrac{4}{3}$ (E) $\dfrac{\sqrt{3}}{4}$

7. Find the area of the region inside the circle $r = \sqrt{3} \sin \theta$
   and outside the cardioid $r = 1 + \cos \theta$.

   7. _____

   (A) $\dfrac{3\sqrt{3}}{4}$ (B) $\dfrac{3\sqrt{3}}{2}$ (C) $\dfrac{\sqrt{3}}{4}$ (D) $\dfrac{\sqrt{3}}{2}$ (E) $\dfrac{3\sqrt{3}}{8}$

Directions: Show all steps leading to your answers, including any intermediate results obtained using a graphing utility. Use the back of the test or another sheet of paper if necessary.

1. A curve is parametrized by $x = t^2 + 5$ and $y = e^{2t}$.

   Find $\dfrac{dy}{dx}$ and $\dfrac{d^2y}{dx^2}$ in terms of t.

2. Find the length of the curve parametrized by
   $x = \dfrac{1}{6}(4t + 1)^{3/2}$, $y = t^2$, $1 \le t \le 5$.

3. A curve is generated by $x = 12t$, $y = \dfrac{1}{2}t^2 + 4$, $5 \le t \le 9$.
   Find the area of the surface generated by revolving the curve about the y-axis.

4. Let $\mathbf{u} = \langle 2, -1 \rangle$ and $\mathbf{v} = \langle -5, 7 \rangle$.
   (a) Find $3\mathbf{u} + \mathbf{v}$.
   (b) Find the magnitude of $3\mathbf{u} + \mathbf{v}$.
   (c) Find $\mathbf{u} \cdot \mathbf{v}$.

5. Find the unit vectors (four vectors in all) that are tangent and normal to the curve $x = 2t^3 - 3t$, $y = -5t^2$, at $t = 2$.

6. An airplane, flying in the direction 35° west of north at 425 mph in still air, encounters a 55-mph wind blowing from the west (i.e., the wind direction is due east). The airplane maintains its air speed and compass heading, but, because of the wind, acquires a new ground speed and direction. What are they?

7. The position vector of a particle in the plane is given by $\mathbf{r}(t) = [\ln(t + 2)]\mathbf{i} + (t^2 - 2)\mathbf{j}$ for $-2 < t \le 2$.

   (a) Draw the graph of the path of the particle.

   (b) Find the velocity and acceleration vectors.

8. Solve the initial value problem for $\mathbf{r}$ as a vector function of t. $\dfrac{d\mathbf{r}}{dt} = (3e^{3t})\mathbf{i} + (2t)\mathbf{j}$, $\mathbf{r}(0) = \mathbf{i} - 4\mathbf{j}$

9. Find the maximum height, the flight time, and the range for an ideal projectile that is launched from the origin at an initial velocity of 50 ft/sec and a launch angle of 40° to the horizontal.

1. $\dfrac{dy}{dx} =$ _____
   $\dfrac{d^2y}{dx^2} =$ _____

2. _____

3. _____

4. (a) _____
   (b) _____
   (c) _____

5. Tangent vectors: _____
   Normal vectors: _____

6. Ground speed: _____
   Direction: _____

7. (a)

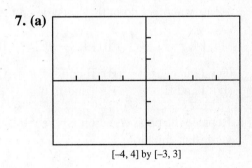

[–4, 4] by [–3, 3]

   (b) $\mathbf{v}(t) =$ _____
       $\mathbf{a}(t) =$ _____

8. _____

9. _____

10. A tennis ball is hit at an angle of 50° to the horizontal
from a height of 1.2 m toward a tall wall that is 11 m away.
If there is no air resistance and the initial velocity is
14 m/sec, at what height does the ball hit the wall?

10. _____

11. Which differential equation describes the motion of a
projectile when a linear drag force (represented by k) is
present? (Assume distance is measured in feet and time is
measured in seconds.)

11. _____

(A) $\dfrac{d\mathbf{r}}{dt} = -32\mathbf{j} - k\mathbf{r}$ (B) $\dfrac{d^2\mathbf{r}}{dt^2} = -32\mathbf{j} + k\dfrac{d\mathbf{r}}{dt}$

(C) $\dfrac{d^2\mathbf{r}}{dt^2} = -32\mathbf{i} + k\dfrac{d\mathbf{r}}{dt}$ (D) $\dfrac{d^2\mathbf{r}}{dt^2} = -k\dfrac{d\mathbf{r}}{dt}$

(E) $\dfrac{d^2\mathbf{r}}{dt^2} = -32\mathbf{j} - k\dfrac{d\mathbf{r}}{dt}$

12. Graph the polar curve given by $r = 1 + 2\cos 2\theta$.

12.

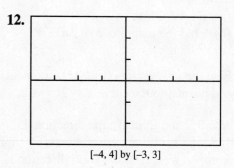

[–4, 4] by [–3, 3]

13. Suppose a polar graph is symmetric about the x-axis and
contains the point $\left(4, \dfrac{\pi}{6}\right)$. Which of the following
identify another point that must be on the graph?

13. _____

   I. $\left(4, -\dfrac{\pi}{6}\right)$ II. $\left(4, \dfrac{5\pi}{6}\right)$ III. $\left(-4, \dfrac{5\pi}{6}\right)$

(A) I only   (B) II only   (C) III only
(D) I and II   (E) I and III

14. Replace the polar equation $r = \sec^2\theta$ by an equivalent
Cartesian equation.

14. _____

15. Find the slope of the polar curve $r = -2\cos 3\theta$ at
$\theta = \dfrac{\pi}{6}$ and at $\theta = \dfrac{\pi}{3}$.

15. At $\dfrac{\pi}{6}$: _____

At $\dfrac{\pi}{3}$: _____

16. Find the area of the region enclosed by the oval limaçon
$r = 5 - 2\cos\theta$.

16. _____

17. Find the length of the polar curve given by $r = 5\sin^2\dfrac{\theta}{2}$
for $0 \le \theta \le \dfrac{\pi}{3}$.

17. _____

Directions: Show all steps leading to your answers, including any intermediate results obtained using a graphing utility. Use the back of the test or another sheet of paper if necessary.

1. A curve is parametrized by $x = e^{3t} + 5$ and $y = t^3 - 4$.

   Find $\dfrac{dy}{dx}$ and $\dfrac{d^2y}{dx^2}$ in terms of t.

   1. $\dfrac{dy}{dx} =$ _____

      $\dfrac{d^2y}{dx^2} =$ _____

2. Find the length of the curve parametrized by
   $x = 3t^2$, $y = \dfrac{1}{18}(12t + 1)^{3/2}$, $1 \le t \le 4$.

   2. _____

3. A curve is generated by $x = \dfrac{1}{2}t^2 + 7$, $y = 8t$, $0 \le t \le 6$.
   Find the area of the surface generated by revolving the curve about the x-axis.

   3. _____

4. Let $\mathbf{u} = \langle -2, 4 \rangle$ and $\mathbf{v} = \langle 3, -5 \rangle$.
   (a) Find $2\mathbf{u} + \mathbf{v}$.
   (b) Find the magnitude of $2\mathbf{u} + \mathbf{v}$.
   (c) Find $\mathbf{u} \cdot \mathbf{v}$.

   4. (a) _____
      (b) _____
      (c) _____

5. Find the unit vectors (four vectors in all) that are tangent and normal to the curve $x = \dfrac{1}{3}t^3 - 2t$, $y = 4t^2$, at $t = 3$.

   5. Tangent vectors: _____

      Normal vectors: _____

6. An airplane, flying in the direction 50° east of north at 375 mph in still air, encounters a 45-mph wind blowing from the north (i.e., the wind direction is due south). The airplane maintains its air speed and compass heading, but, because of the wind, acquires a new ground speed and direction. What are they?

   6. Ground speed: _____

      Direction: _____

7. The position vector of a particle in the plane is given by
   $\mathbf{r}(t) = (t^3 - 3)\mathbf{i} + (e^{-2t} + 2t - 3)\mathbf{j}$ for $-1 \le t \le 2$.

   (a) Draw the graph of the path of the particle.

   (b) Find the velocity and acceleration vectors.

   7. (a)

   [−4, 4] by [−3, 3]

   (b) $\mathbf{v}(t) =$ _____

      $\mathbf{a}(t) =$ _____

8. Solve the initial value problem for $\mathbf{r}$ as a vector function
   of t. $\dfrac{d\mathbf{r}}{dt} = (3t^2)\mathbf{i} + [-\sin(t - 1)]\mathbf{j}$, $\mathbf{r}(1) = 5\mathbf{i} + \mathbf{j}$

   8. _____

9. Find the maximum height, the flight time, and the range for an ideal projectile that is launched from the origin at an initial velocity of 70 ft/sec and a launch angle of 35° to the horizontal.

   9. _____

10. A tennis ball is hit at an angle of 55° to the horizontal   **10.** _____
from a height of 1.4 m toward a tall wall that is 13 m away.
If there is no air resistance and the initial velocity is
12 m/sec, at what height does the ball hit the wall?

11. Which differential equation describes the motion of a   **11.** _____
projectile when a linear drag force (represented by k) is
present? (Assume distance is measured in meters and time
is measured in seconds.)

(A) $\dfrac{d^2\mathbf{r}}{dt^2} = -9.8\mathbf{i} - k\dfrac{d\mathbf{r}}{dt}$ (B) $\dfrac{d^2\mathbf{r}}{dt^2} = -k\dfrac{d\mathbf{r}}{dt}$

(C) $\dfrac{d^2\mathbf{r}}{dt^2} = -9.8\mathbf{j} - k\dfrac{d\mathbf{r}}{dt}$ (D) $\dfrac{d^2\mathbf{r}}{dt^2} = -9.8\mathbf{j} + k\dfrac{d\mathbf{r}}{dt}$

(E) $\dfrac{d\mathbf{r}}{dt} = -9.8\mathbf{j} - k\mathbf{r}$

12. Graph the polar curve given by $r = 1 + 2\sin 3\theta$.   **12.**

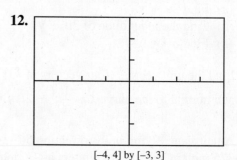

[−4, 4] by [−3, 3]

13. Suppose a polar graph is symmetric about the y-axis and   **13.** _____
contains the point $\left(3, \dfrac{\pi}{3}\right)$. Which of the following
identify another point that must be on the graph?

I. $\left(3, \dfrac{4\pi}{3}\right)$ II. $\left(3, \dfrac{2\pi}{3}\right)$ III. $\left(-3, \dfrac{2\pi}{3}\right)$

(A) I only   (B) II only   (C) III only
(D) I and II   (E) I and III

14. Replace the polar equation $r = \sec\theta\csc\theta$ by an   **14.** _____
equivalent Cartesian equation.

15. Find the slope of the polar curve $r = 3\sin 6\theta$ at   **15.** At $\dfrac{\pi}{4}$: _____
$\theta = \dfrac{\pi}{4}$ and at $\theta = \dfrac{\pi}{3}$.   At $\dfrac{\pi}{3}$: _____

16. Find the area of the region enclosed by the oval limaçon   **16.** _____
$r = 4 + 3\sin\theta$.

17. Find the length of the polar curve given by $r = 3\cos^2\dfrac{\theta}{2}$ **17.** _____
for $0 \le \theta \le \dfrac{\pi}{2}$.

Directions: Show all steps leading to your answers, including any intermediate results obtained using a graphing utility. Use the back of the test or another sheet of paper if necessary.

1. Let $f(x) = \begin{cases} x^2 + 5, & x \le 2 \\ \dfrac{4x - 3}{x + 3}, & x > 2 \end{cases}$.

Find the limit of $f(x)$ as **(a)** $x \to -\infty$, **(b)** $x \to 2^-$, **(c)** $x \to 2^+$, and **(d)** $x \to \infty$

1. (a) _____

   (b) _____
   (c) _____
   (d) _____

2. Find the equations of all lines tangent to $y = x^2 - 4$ that pass through the point $(5, 5)$.

2. _____

3. Find $\dfrac{dy}{dx}$, where $y = x^4 - 5x^3 + 2x$.

3. _____

4. Find $\dfrac{dy}{dx}$, where $y = \dfrac{x^2 - 5}{\cos x}$

4. _____

5. Use implicit differentiation to find $\dfrac{dy}{dx}$ if $x^2(3y - 5) = y^3 - x$.

5. _____

6. Find $\dfrac{dy}{dx}$ if $y = 4^{-x}$.

   (A) $(-x)(4^{-x-1})$ (B) -4^{-x} (C) $(\ln 4)^{-x}$
   (D) $(\ln 4)(4^{-x})$ (E) $(-\ln 4)(4^{-x})$

6. _____

7. The graph below represents the *derivative* of a function f, where $f(-1) = -2$. Sketch a possible graph of $y = f(x)$.

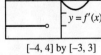

$y = f'(x)$

$[-4, 4]$ by $[-3, 3]$

7.

$[-4, 4]$ by $[-3, 3]$

8. For $y = x - 3e^{-x^2}$, use graphing techniques with analytical support to find the approximate intervals on which the function is

   (a) increasing,   **(b)** decreasing,
   (c) concave up,   **(d)** concave down.
   Then find any
   (e) local extreme values,   **(f)** inflection points.

8. (a) _____
   (b) _____

   (c) _____
   (d) _____
   (e) Min: _____ at $x \approx$ _____
   Max: _____ at $x \approx$ _____
   (f) _____

9. Use the graph of the function *f* to estimate where **(a)** f' and **(b)** f'' are 0, positive, and negative.

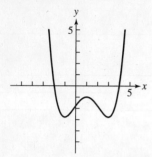

9. (a) $f' = 0$: _____
           $f' > 0$: _____
           $f' < 0$: _____
    (b) $f'' = 0$: _____
           $f'' > 0$: _____
           $f'' < 0$: _____

10. You are planning to make an open box from a 30- by 42-inch piece of sheet metal by cutting congruent squares from the corners and folding up the sides. You want the box to have the largest possible volume.

   (a) What size square should you cut from each corner? (Give the side length of the square.)
   (b) What is the largest possible volume your box will have?

10. (a) _____
     (b) _____

11. Find the linearization $L(x)$ of $f(x) = 3x^4 - 5x^3$ at $x = 2$.

   (A) $L(x) = 8x - 8$ (B) $L(x) = 32x - 56$
   (C) $L(x) = 36x$ (D) $L(x) = 36x + 8$
   (E) $L(x) = 36x - 64$

11. _____

12. You are using Newton's method to solve $\ln x - 3 = 0$. If your first guess is $x_1 = 15$, what value will you calculate for the next approximation x_2?

12. _____

13. Suppose that the edge lengths *x*, *y*, and *z* of a closed rectangular box are changing at the following rates:
$$\frac{dx}{dt} = 4 \text{ ft/sec}, \frac{dy}{dt} = 0 \text{ ft/sec}, \frac{dz}{dt} = -3 \text{ ft/sec}.$$
Find the rates at which the box's **(a)** volume, **(b)** surface area, and **(c)** diagonal length $s = \sqrt{x^2 + y^2 + z^2}$ are changing at the instant when $x = 10$ ft, $y = 8$ ft, and $z = 5$ ft.

13. (a) _____
     (b) _____
     (c) _____

14. The table below shows the velocity of a car in an amusement park ride during the first 24 seconds of the ride. Use the left-endpoint values (LRAM) to estimate the distance traveled, using 6 intervals of length 4.

14. _____

Time (sec)	0	4	8	12	16	20	24
Velocity (ft/sec)	0	4	7	7	11	16	18

A **Chapters 1–7** *(continued)* NAME _____

15. Express the limit as a definite integral.

$$\lim_{\|P\| \to 0} \sum_{k=1}^{n} \left(2c_k + \frac{1}{c_k^2}\right) \Delta x, \text{ where } P \text{ is any partition of}$$

$[7, 15]$.

15. _____

16. Consider the integral $\int_0^4 (x^2 - 3x + 5)\, dx$.

  (a) Estimate the value of the integral using
  4 right-endpoint rectangles (RRAM).
  (b) Estimate the value of the integral using the
  Trapezoidal Rule with $n = 4$.
  (c) Integrate to find the exact value of the integral.

16. **(a)** _____
  (b) _____
  (c) _____

17. Suppose that f and g are continuous and that $\int_{-1}^{4} f(x)\, dx = 5$,

$\int_{-1}^{4} g(x)\, dx = -2$, and $\int_{1}^{4} g(x)\, dx = 3$. Find each integral.

  (a) $\int_{-1}^{4} [f(x) - g(x)]\, dx$ **(b)** $\int_{-1}^{4} [3f(x) + 5g(x)]\, dx$

  (c) $\int_{-1}^{1} g(x)\, dx$

17. **(a)** _____
  (b) _____
  (c) _____

18. Find the average value of the
function $g(x) = 2 + \sqrt{9 - x^2}$
on the interval $[-3, 3]$ without
integrating, by appealing to
the region between the graph
and the x-axis.

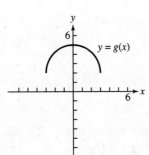

18. _____

19. Use NINT to evaluate $\int_{-1.7}^{2.6} \frac{5 \cos x}{e^x + x^2}\, dx$.

19. _____

20. Find $\dfrac{d}{dx} \int_0^{2x} (5 - t)\, dt$.

20. _____

21. Evaluate each integral using Part 2 of the Fundamental

  Theorem of Calculus.

  (a) $\int_{-1}^{3} (3x^2 - 12x + 4)\, dx$ **(b)** $\int_{1}^{16} x^{3/4} dx$

  (c) $\int_{\pi/2}^{5\pi/6} \csc \theta \cot \theta \, d\theta$

21. **(a)** _____
  (b) _____
  (c) _____

22. Find $\dfrac{dy}{dx}$ if $y = \int_1^{x^2} (3t^2 - 5t)\, dt$.

  (A) $3x^2 - 5x$ **(B)** $6x^3 - 10x^2$ **(C)** $12x^3 - 10x$
  (D) $6x^5 - 10x^3$ **(E)** $3x^6 - 5x^4$

22. _____

23. Use the Trapezoidal Rule with $n = 6$ to approximate the value of $\int_0^3 e^x\, dx$

    23. _____

24. Use the Fundamental Theorem of Calculus to evaluate $\int \sqrt{5 - \sin x}\, dx$.

    24. _____

    (A) $-\dfrac{\cos x}{2\sqrt{5 - \sin x}} + C$

    (B) $\int_0^x \sqrt{5 - \sin t}\, dt + C$

    (C) $\int_x^0 \sqrt{5 - \sin t}\, dt + C$

    (D) $\int_0^x \dfrac{-\cos x}{2\sqrt{5 - \sin x}} + C$

    (E) $\dfrac{2}{3}(5 - \sin x)^{3/2} + C$

25. Evaluate the integral.

    $\int \left(x^4 - \dfrac{4}{x^2} + e^{2x} \right) dx$

    25. _____

26. Solve the initial value problem.

    $\dfrac{dy}{dx} = (3x - 4)^3,\ y(1) = -1$

    26. _____

27. Suppose $y = f(x)$ is a solution to the differential equation whose slope field is shown. Sketch a possible graph for the function f satisfying $f(0) = 1$.

    27.

    [−4, 4] by [−3, 3]

28. Use substitution to evaluate the integral.

    $\int \sqrt{\tan^5 x}\ \sec^2 x\, dx$

    28. _____

29. Solve the differential equation by separation of variables.

    $\dfrac{dy}{dx} = \dfrac{x \cos (x^2)}{y^2 - 2}$

    29. _____

30. Use integration by parts to evaluate $\int x \sin (2x - 5)\, dx$.

    30. _____

31. Use tabular integration or another method to evaluate the integral.

$$\int x^3 e^{-2x} \, dx$$

31. _____

32. Suppose a certain element has a half-life of 4.6 weeks. If a sample contains 300 grams of this element, how much of it will remain after 7 weeks?

32. _____

33. The table gives the growth of a population of wild deer. Let $x = 0$ represent 1950, $x = 10$ represent 1960, and so forth.

Year	1950	1960	1970	1980	1990
Population	152	352	580	716	775

(a) Find the logistic regression equation for the data and superimpose its graph on a scatter plot of the data.
(b) Find the carrying capacity predicted by the regression equation.
(c) Find when the rate of growth predicted by the regression equation changes from increasing to decreasing. Estimate the population at this time.

33. (a)

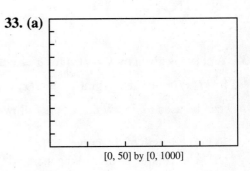

[0, 50] by [0, 1000]

(b) _____

(c) Year: _____

Population: _____

34. The function $v(t) = 2t - 4$ is the velocity in ft/sec of a particle moving along the x-axis for $0 \le t \le 8$. Use analytic methods to answer the following questions.

(a) Determine when the particle is moving to the right, to the left, and stopped.
(b) Find the particle's displacement for the given time interval.
(c) Find the total distance traveled by the particle.

34. (a) Right: _____

Left: _____

Stopped: _____

(b) _____

(c) _____

35. At a certain paint factory, the production rate in gallons per hour x hours after the factory opens in the morning is given by the function

$r(x) = -\dfrac{3}{5}x^4 + 16x^3 - 135x^2 + 400x$. How much paint is produced during the first 3 hours after opening?

35. _____

36. Find the area of the shaded region analytically.   36. _____

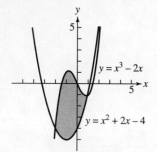

$y = x^3 - 2x$

$y = x^2 + 2x - 4$

37. A curve is given by $y = f(x)$ for $a \le x \le b$, where $a > 0$ 37. _____
and $f(x) > 0$. The integral $\int_a^b 2\pi f(x)\sqrt{1 + (f'(x))^2}\, dx$
can be used to find which of the following?

(A) The length of the curve
(B) The volume of the solid generated by revolving the
the region below the curve about the x-axis
(C) The volume of the solid generated by revolving the
region below the curve about the y-axis
(D) The area of the surface generated by revolving the
curve about the x-axis
(E) The area of the surface generated by revolving the
curve about the y-axis

38. A region is bounded by the line $y = x$ and the parabola   38. _____
$y = x^2 - 6x + 10$. Find the volume of the solid generated
by revolving the region about the x-axis.

39. The base of a solid is the region between the x-axis and   39. _____
the graph of $y = \sec x$ for $-\dfrac{\pi}{3} < x < \dfrac{\pi}{3}$. Each cross
section perpendicular to the x-axis is an isosceles right
triangle with its hypotenuse in the xy-plane. Find the
volume of the solid.

40. Find the length of the curve described by $y = \dfrac{4}{3}x^{3/2}$ for   40. _____
$0 \le x \le 6$.

41. A spring has a natural length of 12 cm. A 40-N force   41. _____
stretches the spring to 16 cm. How much work is done in
stretching the spring from 12 cm to 24 cm?

Directions: Show all steps leading to your answers, including any intermediate results obtained using a graphing utility. Use the back of the test or another sheet of paper if necessary.

1. Let $f(x) = \begin{cases} \dfrac{6x + 4}{x - 6}, & x < 1 \\ 2 - x^3, & x \geq 1 \end{cases}$.

Find the limit of $f(x)$ as **(a)** $x \to -\infty$, **(b)** $x \to 1^-$, **(c)** $x \to 1^+$, and **(d)** $x \to \infty$

1. (a) _____

(b) _____

(c) _____

(d) _____

2. Find the equations of all lines tangent to $y = x^2 - 6$ that pass through the point $(4, 6)$.

2. _____

3. Find $\dfrac{dy}{dx}$, where $y = x^6 + 8x^2 - 11x$.

3. _____

4. Find $\dfrac{dy}{dx}$, where $y = \dfrac{\sin x}{x^2 + 3}$.

4. _____

5. Use implicit differentiation to find $\dfrac{dy}{dx}$ if $4y(x^3 + 2) = 5y^3 + x$.

5. _____

6. Find $\dfrac{dy}{dx}$ if $y = 3^{2.5x}$.

(A) $(\ln 2.5)3^{2.5x}$ (B) $2.5(3^{2.5x})$ (C) $(\ln 3)(3^{2.5x})$
(D) $2.5(\ln 3)(3^{2.5x})$ (E) $(2.5x)(3^{1.5x})$

6. _____

7. The graph below represents the *derivative* of a function f, where $f(1) = -1$. Sketch a possible graph of $y = f(x)$.

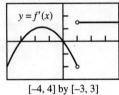

[–4, 4] by [–3, 3]

7.

[–4, 4] by [–3, 3]

8. For $y = 2x - 5e^{-x^2}$, use graphing techniques with analytical support to find the approximate intervals on which the function is

(a) increasing,   **(b)** decreasing,
(c) concave up,   **(d)** concave down.

Then find any

(e) local extreme values,   **(f)** inflection points.

8. (a) _____

(b) _____

(c) _____

(d) _____

(e) Min: _____ at $x \approx$ _____

Max: _____ at $x \approx$ _____

(f) _____

9. Use the graph of the function f to estimate where **(a)** f' and **(b)** f'' are 0, positive, and negative.

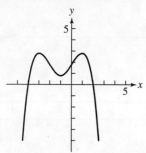

9. (a) $f' = 0$: _____

$f' > 0$: _____

$f' < 0$: _____

(b) $f'' = 0$: _____

$f'' > 0$: _____

$f'' < 0$: _____

10. You are planning to make an open box from a 24- by 32-inch piece of sheet metal by cutting congruent squares from the corners and folding up the sides. You want the box to have the largest possible volume.

   (a) What size square should you cut from each corner? (Give the side length of the square.)

   (b) What is the largest possible volume your box will have?

10. (a) _____

(b) _____

11. Find the linearization $L(x)$ of $f(x) = 2x^4 - 40x^2 + 100$ at $x = 3$.

   (A) $L(x) = -24x$ (B) $L(x) = -24x - 26$
   (C) $L(x) = -24x - 98$ (D) $L(x) = -98x$
   (E) $L(x) = -21x - 35$

11. _____

12. You are using Newton's method to solve $e^x - 2$. If your first guess is $x_1 = 1$, what value will you calculate for the next approximation x_2?

12. _____

13. Suppose that the edge lengths x, y, and z of a closed rectangular box are changing at the following rates:

   $\frac{dx}{dt} = 2$ ft/sec, $\frac{dy}{dt} = -5$ ft/sec, $\frac{dz}{dt} = 0$ ft/sec.

   Find the rates at which the box's **(a)** volume, **(b)** surface area, and **(c)** diagonal length $s = \sqrt{x^2 + y^2 + z^2}$ are changing at the instant when $x = 7$ ft, $y = 4$ ft, and $z = 9$ ft.

13. (a) _____

(b) _____

(c) _____

14. The table below shows the velocity of a running dog during a 35-second time interval. Use the right-endpoint values (RRAM) to estimate the distance traveled, using 7 intervals of length 5.

14. _____

Time (sec)	0	5	10	15	20	25	30	35
Velocity (ft/sec)	18	22	28	27	25	26	28	30

B **Chapters 1–7** (continued)   NAME

15. Express the limit as a definite integral.

    $$\lim_{\|P\|\to 0} \sum_{k=1}^{n} \left(5c_k^2 - \frac{3}{c_k}\right) \Delta x,$$ where P is any partition of

    $[3, 11]$.

16. Consider the integral $\int_0^5 (x^2 + 2x - 4)\, dx$.

    (a) Estimate the value of the integral using
        5 left-endpoint rectangles (LRAM).
    (b) Estimate the value of the integral using the
        Trapezoidal Rule with $n = 5$.
    (c) Integrate to find the exact value of the integral.

17. Suppose that f and g are continuous and that $\int_{-2}^{5} f(x)\, dx = 3$,

    $\int_{-2}^{3} f(x)\, dx = 7$, and $\int_{-2}^{3} g(x)\, dx = -8$. Find each integral.

    (a) $\int_{3}^{5} f(x)\, dx$ (b) $\int_{-2}^{3} [f(x) + g(x)]\, dx$

    (c) $\int_{-2}^{3} [4g(x) - 5f(x)]\, dx$

18. Find the average value of the
    function $g(x) = 5 - \sqrt{16 - x^2}$
    on the interval $[-4, 4]$ without
    integrating, by appealing to
    the region between the graph
    and the x-axis.

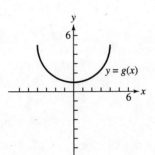

19. Use NINT to evaluate $\int_{-5.2}^{1.2} \frac{2e^x}{x^2 + \cos x}\, dx$.

20. Find $\dfrac{d}{dx} \int_0^{3x} (2t - 7)\, dt$.

21. Evaluate each integral using Part 2 of the Fundamental
    Theorem of Calculus.

    (a) $\int_{-2}^{4} (5x^2 + 14x - 3)\, dx$ (b) $\int_{1}^{8} x^{2/3} dx$

    (c) $\int_{\pi/3}^{2\pi/3} \csc^2\theta\, d\theta$

22. Find $\dfrac{dy}{dx}$ if $y = \int_{1}^{x^3} (6t^2 - 7)\, dt$.

    (A) $18x^4 - 21x^2$ (B) $12x^5 - 7x^3$ (C) $12x^5 - 21x^2$
    (D) $6x^6 - 7$ (E) $18x^8 - 21x^2$

15. _____

16. (a) _____
    (b) _____
    (c) _____

17. (a) _____
    (b) _____
    (c) _____

18. _____

19. _____

20. _____

21. (a) _____
    (b) _____
    (c) _____

22. _____

23. Use the Trapezoidal Rule with $n = 6$ to approximate the value of $\int_{2}^{4} 5 \ln x \, dx$.

23. _____

24. Use the Fundamental Theorem of Calculus to evaluate $\int \sin \sqrt{x + 7} \, dx$.

24. _____

    (A) $-\cos x \sqrt{x + 7} + C$

    (B) $\int_{0}^{x} \dfrac{\cos \sqrt{t + 7}}{2\sqrt{t + 7}} \, dt + C$

    (C) $\dfrac{\cos \sqrt{x + 7}}{2\sqrt{x + 7}} + C$

    (D) $\int_{x}^{0} \sin \sqrt{t + 7} \, dt + C$

    (E) $\int_{0}^{x} \sin \sqrt{t + 7} \, dt + C$

25. Evaluate the integral.

$$\int \left(3x^5 - \frac{1}{x^3} + e^{7x} \right) dx$$

25. _____

26. Solve the initial value problem.

$$\frac{dy}{dx} = (-5x + 7)^2, \, y(1) = -1$$

26. _____

27. Suppose $y = f(x)$ is a solution to the differential equation whose slope field is shown. Sketch a possible graph for the function f satisfying $f(0) = -2$.

27.

[–4, 4] by [–3, 3]

28. Use substitution to evaluate the integral.

$$\int \sec^5 x \tan x \, dx$$

28. _____

29. Solve the differential equation by separation of variables.

$$\frac{dy}{dx} = \frac{x + 7}{3y^2 \sin (y^3)}$$

29. _____

30. Use integration by parts to evaluate $\int x \cos (3x + 4) \, dx$.

30. _____

31. Use tabular integration or another method to evaluate the integral.

$$\int x^2 e^{-5x}\, dx$$

31. _____

32. Suppose a certain element has a half-life of 6.3 days. If a sample contains 700 grams of this element, how much of it will remain after 16 days?

32. _____

33. The table gives the growth of a population of coyotes. Let $x = 0$ represent 1950, $x = 10$ represent 1960, and so forth.

Year	1950	1960	1970	1980	1990
Population	23	102	325	553	642

(a) Find the logistic regression equation for the data and superimpose its graph on a scatter plot of the data.
(b) Find the carrying capacity predicted by the regression equation.
(c) Find when the rate of growth predicted by the regression equation changes from increasing to decreasing. Estimate the population at this time.

33. (a)

[0, 50] by [0, 1000]

(b) _____

(c) Year: _____
   Population: _____

34. The function $v(t) = 9 - 3t$ is the velocity in ft/sec of a particle moving along the x-axis for $0 \le t \le 10$. Use analytic methods to answer the following questions.

(a) Determine when the particle is moving to the right, to the left, and stopped.
(b) Find the particle's displacement for the given time interval.
(c) Find the total distance traveled by the particle.

34. (a) Right: _____
   Left: _____
   Stopped: _____

(b) _____
(c) _____

35. At a certain glue factory, the production rate in gallons per hour x hours after the factory opens in the morning is given by the function

$r(x) = -\dfrac{1}{2}x^4 + 12x^3 - 105x^2 + 400x.$ How much glue is produced during the first 5 hours after opening?

35. _____

36. Find the area of the shaded region analytically.   **36.** _____

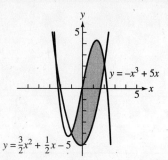

$y = -x^3 + 5x$

$y = \frac{3}{2}x^2 + \frac{1}{2}x - 5$

37. A curve is given by $y = f(x)$ for $a \le x \le b$, where $a > 0$ **37.** _____

and $f(x) > 0$. The integral $\displaystyle\int_a^b 2\pi x \cdot f(x)\, dx$

can be used to find which of the following?

(A) The length of the curve
(B) The volume of the solid generated by revolving the
    the region below the curve about the x-axis
(C) The volume of the solid generated by revolving the
    region below the curve about the y-axis
(D) The area of the surface generated by revolving the
    curve about the x-axis
(E) The area of the surface generated by revolving the
    curve about the y-axis

38. A region is bounded by the line $y = 10 - x$ and the   **38.** _____
parabola $y = x^2 - 6x + 10$. Find the volume of the solid
generated by revolving the region about the x-axis.

39. The base of a solid is the region between the x-axis and   **39.** _____

the graph of $y = \sqrt{\sin^3 x}$ for $0 \le x \le \dfrac{\pi}{2}$. Each cross

section perpendicular to the x-axis is a rectangle whose

base is in the xy-plane and whose other side has length

$\cos x$. Find the volume of the solid.

40. Find the length of the curve described by $y = 2x^{3/2}$ for   **40.** _____

$0 \le x \le 7$.

41. A spring has a natural length of 14 cm. A 24-N force   **41.** _____
stretches the spring to 17 cm. How much work is done in
stretching the spring from 14 cm to 20 cm?

Directions: Show all steps leading to your answers, including any intermediate results obtained using a graphing utility. Use the back of the test or another sheet of paper if necessary.

1. Let $f(x) = \begin{cases} x^2 + 5, & x \le 2 \\ \dfrac{4x - 3}{x + 3}, & x > 2 \end{cases}$.

Find the limit of $f(x)$ as **(a)** $x \to -\infty$, **(b)** $x \to 2^-$, **(c)** $x \to 2^+$, and **(d)** $x \to \infty$

1. (a) _____

(b) _____

(c) _____

(d) _____

2. Find the equations of all lines tangent to $y = x^2 - 4$ that pass through the point $(5, 5)$.

2. _____

3. Find $\dfrac{dy}{dx}$, where $y = \dfrac{x^2 - 5}{\cos x}$.

3. _____

4. Use implicit differentiation to find $\dfrac{dy}{dx}$ if $x^2(3y - 5) = y^3 - x$.

4. _____

5. Find $\dfrac{dy}{dx}$ if $y = 4^{-x}$.

(A) $(-x)(4^{-x-1})$ (B) -4^{-x} (C) $(\ln 4)^{-x}$
(D) $(\ln 4)(4^{-x})$ (E) $(-\ln 4)(4^{-x})$

5. _____

6. For $y = x - 3e^{-x^2}$, use graphing techniques with analytical support to find the approximate intervals on which the function is

(a) increasing, **(b)** decreasing,
(c) concave up, **(d)** concave down.

Then find any

(e) local extreme values, **(f)** inflection points.

6. (a) _____
(b) _____

(c) _____
(d) _____
(e) Min: _____ at $x \approx$ _____
   Max: _____ at $x \approx$ _____

(f) _____

7. You are planning to make an open box from a 30- by 42-inch piece of sheet metal by cutting congruent squares from the corners and folding up the sides. You want the box to have the largest possible volume.

(a) What size square should you cut from each corner? (Give the side length of the square.)
(b) What is the largest possible volume your box will have?

7. (a) _____
(b) _____

8. Consider the integral $\int_0^4 (x^2 - 3x + 5)\, dx$.

    8. (a) _____

    (b) _____

    (c) _____

  (a) Estimate the value of the integral using
4 right-endpoint rectangles (RRAM).

  (b) Estimate the value of the integral using the
Trapezoidal Rule with $n = 4$.

  (c) Integrate to find the exact value of the integral.

9. Find $\dfrac{d}{dx} \int_0^{2x} (5 - t)\, dt$.

    9. _____

10. Use the Fundamental Theorem of Calculus to evaluate
$\int \sqrt{5 - \sin x}\, dx$.

    10. _____

  (A) $-\dfrac{\cos x}{2\sqrt{5 - \sin x}} + C$

  (B) $\int_0^x \sqrt{5 - \sin t}\, dt + C$

  (C) $\int_x^0 \sqrt{5 - \sin t}\, dt + C$

  (D) $\int_0^x \dfrac{-\cos x}{2\sqrt{5 - \sin x}} + C$

  (E) $\dfrac{2}{3}(5 - \sin x)^{3/2} + C$

11. Solve the initial value problem.
$$\frac{dy}{dx} = (3x - 4)^3, \; y(1) = -1$$

    11. _____

12. Solve the differential equation by separation of variables.
$$\frac{dy}{dx} = \frac{x \cos (x^2)}{y^2 - 2}$$

    12. _____

13. Use integration by parts to evaluate $\int x \sin (2x - 5)\, dx$.

    13. _____

14. Suppose a certain element has a half-life of 4.6 weeks.
If a sample contains 300 grams of this element, how much
of it will remain after 7 weeks?

    14. _____

15. The table gives the growth of a population of wild deer. Let $x = 0$ represent 1950, $x = 10$ represent 1960, and so forth.

Year	1950	1960	1970	1980	1990
Population	152	352	580	716	775

   (a) Find the logistic regression equation for the data and superimpose its graph on a scatter plot of the data.
   (b) Find the carrying capacity predicted by the regression equation.
   (c) Find when the rate of growth predicted by the regression equation changes from increasing to decreasing. Estimate the population at this time.

15. (a)

[0, 50] by [0, 1000]

(b) _____
(c) Year: _____
   Population: _____

16. Use Euler's method to solve the initial value problem graphically staring at $x_0 = 0$ with $dx = 0.1$. (Use a smooth curve to indicate the approximate solution.)

$$y' = -\frac{1}{4}(x + y^3), \quad y(0) = 1$$

16.

[0, 8] by [–3, 3]

17. The function $v(t) = 2t - 4$ is the velocity in ft/sec of a particle moving along the x-axis for $0 \le t \le 8$. Use analytic methods to answer the following questions.

   (a) Determine when the particle is moving to the right, to the left, and stopped.
   (b) Find the particle's displacement for the given time interval.
   (c) Find the total distance traveled by the particle.

17. (a) Right: _____
   Left: _____
   Stopped: _____
(b) _____
(c) _____

18. Find the area of the shaded region analytically.

18. _____

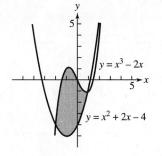

$y = x^3 - 2x$

$y = x^2 + 2x - 4$

---

19. A curve is given by $y = f(x)$ for $a \leq x \leq b$, where $a > 0$ and $f(x) > 0$. The integral $\int_a^b 2\pi f(x)\sqrt{1 + (f'(x))^2}\, dx$ can be used to find which of the following?

    (A) The length of the curve

    (B) The volume of the solid generated by revolving the the region below the curve about the x-axis

    (C) The volume of the solid generated by revolving the region below the curve about the y-axis

    (D) The area of the surface generated by revolving the curve about the x-axis

    (E) The area of the surface generated by revolving the curve about the y-axis

19. _____

20. A region is bounded by the line $y = x$ and the parabola $y = x^2 - 6x + 10$. Find the volume of the solid generated by revolving the region about the x-axis.

20. _____

21. Find the length of the curve described by $y = \frac{4}{3}x^{3/2}$ for $0 \leq x \leq 6$.

21. _____

22. A spring has a natural length of 12 cm. A 40-N force stretches the spring to 16 cm. How much work is done in stretching the spring from 12 cm to 24 cm?

22. _____

23. Use l'Hôpital's rule to evaluate each limit.

    (a) $\lim\limits_{x \to 3} \dfrac{x^3 - 2x^2 - 5x + 6}{x^2 + 2x - 15}$

    (b) $\lim\limits_{x \to \infty} \left(1 + \dfrac{2}{5x}\right)^{3x}$

23. (a) _____

    (b) _____

24. Order the functions from the slowest-growing to fastest-growing as $x \to \infty$.
$$5x^2, \ x^3, \ \ln(x + 3), \ e^{x/2}$$

24. _____

25. Evaluate the improper integral $\int_2^\infty \dfrac{dx}{x(\ln x)^4}$ or state that it diverges.

25. _____

26. Which expression with undetermined coefficients should   26. _____
be used to express $\dfrac{(x-2)^2}{(x-1)^2(x^2+3)}$ as a sum of partial
fractions?

(A) $\dfrac{A}{x-1} + \dfrac{B}{(x-1)^2} + \dfrac{Cx+D}{x^2+3}$

(B) $\dfrac{A}{x-1} + \dfrac{B}{(x-1)^2} + \dfrac{C}{x+3} + \dfrac{D}{x^2+3}$

(C) $\dfrac{Ax+B}{(x-1)^2} + \dfrac{Cx+D}{x^2+3}$

(D) $\dfrac{A(x-2)}{x-1} + \dfrac{B(x-2)^2}{(x-1)^2} + \dfrac{(Cx+D)(x-2)^2}{x^2+3}$

(E) $\dfrac{Ax+B}{x-1} + \dfrac{Cx+D}{(x-1)^2} + \dfrac{Ex+F}{x^2+3}$

27. Evaluate $\displaystyle\int \dfrac{4x^3 - 69x - 83}{(x+1)(x-5)}\,dx$.   27. _____

28. Tell whether the series converges or diverges. If it   28. _____
converges, find its sum.

$$5 - \frac{15}{4} + \frac{45}{16} - \frac{135}{64} + \cdots + 5\left(-\frac{3}{4}\right)^n + \cdots$$

29. Find the Maclaurin series for xe^{2x}.   29. _____

30. Let $f(x) = (3x-2)^8$. Use the Remainder Estimation   30. _____
Theorem to estimate the maximum absolute error when
$f(x)$ is replaced by $256 - 3072x$ for $|x| \le 0.04$.

31. Determine the convergence or divergence of the series   31. _____
$\displaystyle\sum_{n=1}^{\infty} \dfrac{n-3}{n^3 + \ln(2n)}$. Identify the test (or tests) you use.

32. Which of the following converge conditionally.   32. _____

I. $\displaystyle\sum_{n=1}^{\infty} (-1)^n \dfrac{1}{\sqrt{n+3}}$

II. $\displaystyle\sum_{n=1}^{\infty} (-1)^n \dfrac{n^2 + 3n - 4}{n!}$

III. $\displaystyle\sum_{n=1}^{\infty} (-1)^n \dfrac{n-2}{n^2+2}$

(A) I only   (B) II only   (C) III only

(D) I and III   (E) II and III

33. Find the interval of convergence of the series   33. _____
$\displaystyle\sum_{n=1}^{\infty} \dfrac{(x-3)^n}{2^n \cdot n}$

34. A wheel of radius 3 rolls along the *x*-axis without slipping. The path traced by a point *P* on the wheel's edge is a cycloid. If *P* is initially at the origin, which of the following pairs of equations represents this cycloid?

(A) $x = 3(1 - \cos t), y = 3(t + \sin t)$
(B) $x = 3(t - \sin t), y = 3(1 - \cos t)$
(C) $x = 3(1 - \sin t), y = 3(t - \cos t)$
(D) $x = 3(t - \sin t), y = 3(1 + \cos t)$
(E) $x = 3(t - \cos t), y = 3(1 + \sin t)$

34. _____

35. A semicircle is defined parametrically by $x = 3 + 2 \sin t$, $y = 2 \cos t, \dfrac{\pi}{3} \le t \le \dfrac{4\pi}{3}$. Find the area of the surface generated by revolving this curve about the *y*-axis.

35. _____

36. Let $\mathbf{u} = \langle 7, -2 \rangle$ and $\mathbf{v} = \langle 3, 5 \rangle$.

(a) Find $3\mathbf{u} - 5\mathbf{v}$.

(b) Find the magnitude of $\mathbf{u}$.

(c) Find $\mathbf{u} \cdot \mathbf{v}$.

36. (a) _____
(b) _____
(c) _____

37. Solve the initial value problem for $\mathbf{r}$ as a vector function of *t*.

$$\frac{d\mathbf{r}}{dt} = (e^{t/2} - 5)\mathbf{i} + (t + 4)^{3/2}\mathbf{j}, \, \mathbf{r}(0) = 7\mathbf{j}$$

37. _____

38. A ball is hit at an angle of 36° to the horizontal from 14 feet above the ground. If it hits the ground 26 feet away (in horizontal distance), what was the initial velocity? Assume there is no air resistance.

38. _____

39. (a) Graph the polar curve $r = 3 \cos 4\theta$.

(b) What is the shortest length a θ-interval can have and still produce the graph?

39. (a)

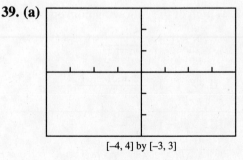

[–4, 4] by [–3, 3]

(b) _____

40. Find the area of the region inside the oval limaçon $r = 2 + \cos \theta$ and outside the oval limaçon $r = 3 - \cos \theta$.

40. _____

Directions: Show all steps leading to your answers, including any intermediate results obtained using a graphing utility. Use the back of the test or another sheet of paper if necessary.

1. Let $f(x) = \begin{cases} \dfrac{6x + 4}{x - 6}, & x < 1 \\ 2 - x^3, & x \geq 1 \end{cases}$.

Find the limit of $f(x)$ as **(a)** $x \to -\infty$, **(b)** $x \to 1^-$,
(c) $x \to 1^+$, and **(d)** $x \to \infty$

1. (a) _____

(b) _____

(c) _____

(d) _____

2. Find the equations of all lines tangent to $y = x^2 - 6$ that pass through the point (4, 6).

2. _____

3. Find $\dfrac{dy}{dx}$, where $y = \dfrac{\sin x}{x^2 + 3}$

3. _____

4. Use implicit differentiation to find $\dfrac{dy}{dx}$ if
$4y(x^3 + 2) = 5y^3 + x$.

4. _____

5. Find $\dfrac{dy}{dx}$ if $y = 3^{2.5x}$.

5. _____

(A) $(\ln 2.5)3^{2.5x}$ (B) $2.5(3^{2.5x})$ (C) $(\ln 3)(3^{2.5x})$
(D) $2.5(\ln 3)(3^{2.5x})$ (E) $(2.5x)(3^{1.5x})$

6. For $y = 2x - 5e^{-x^2}$, use graphing techniques with analytical support to find the approximate intervals on which the function is

(a) increasing,   **(b)** decreasing,
(c) concave up,   **(d)** concave down.
Then find any
(e) local extreme values,   **(f)** inflection points.

6. (a) _____

(b) _____

(c) _____

(d) _____

(e) Min: _____ at $x \approx$ _____

Max: _____ at $x \approx$ _____

(f) _____

7. You are planning to make an open box from a 24- by 32-inch piece of sheet metal by cutting congruent squares from the corners and folding up the sides. You want the box to have the largest possible volume.

7. (a) _____

(b) _____

(a) What size square should you cut from each corner? (Give the side length of the square.)
(b) What is the largest possible volume your box will have?

8. Consider the integral $\int_0^5 (x^2 + 2x - 4)\, dx$.   8. (a) _____
   (a) Estimate the value of the integral using   (b) _____
       5 left-endpoint rectangles (LRAM).   (c) _____
   (b) Estimate the value of the integral using the
       Trapezoidal Rule with $n = 5$.
   (c) Integrate to find the exact value of the integral.

9. Find $\dfrac{d}{dx} \int_0^{3x} (2t - 7)\, dt$.   9. _____

10. Use the Fundamental Theorem of Calculus to evaluate   10. _____
   $\int \sin \sqrt{x + 7}\, dx$.

   (A) $-\cos x \sqrt{x + 7} + C$

   (B) $\int_0^x \dfrac{\cos \sqrt{t + 7}}{2\sqrt{t + 7}}\, dt + C$

   (C) $\dfrac{\cos \sqrt{x + 7}}{2\sqrt{x + 7}} + C$

   (D) $\int_x^0 \sin \sqrt{t + 7}\, dt + C$

   (E) $\int_0^x \sin \sqrt{t + 7}\, dt + C$

11. Solve the initial value problem.   11. _____
   $\dfrac{dy}{dx} = (-5x + 7)^2,\ y(1) = -1$

12. Solve the differential equation by separation of variables.   12. _____
   $\dfrac{dy}{dx} = \dfrac{x + 7}{3y^2 \sin(y^3)}$

13. Use integration by parts to evaluate $\int x \cos(3x + 4)\, dx$.   13. _____

14. Suppose a certain element has a half-life of 6.3 days.   14. _____
   If a sample contains 700 grams of this element, how much
   of it will remain after 16 days?

15. The table gives the growth of a population of coyotes. Let $x = 0$ represent 1950, $x = 10$ represent 1960, and so forth.

Year	1950	1960	1970	1980	1990
Population	23	102	325	553	642

   (a) Find the logistic regression equation for the data and superimpose its graph on a scatter plot of the data.

   (b) Find the carrying capacity predicted by the regression equation.

   (c) Find when the rate of growth predicted by the regression equation changes from increasing to decreasing. Estimate the population at this time.

15. (a)

[0, 50] by [0, 1000]

   (b) _____

   (c) Year: _____
   Population: _____

16. Use Euler's method to solve the initial value problem graphically staring at $x_0 = 0$ with $dx = 0.1$. (Use a smooth curve to indicate the approximate solution.)

$$y' = 2 - \frac{1}{2}x - 2y, \quad y(0) = -2$$

16.

[0, 8] by [–3, 3]

17. The function $v(t) = 9 - 3t$ is the velocity in ft/sec of a particle moving along the x-axis for $0 \le t \le 10$. Use analytic methods to answer the following questions.

   (a) Determine when the particle is moving to the right, to the left, and stopped.

   (b) Find the particle's displacement for the given time interval.

   (c) Find the total distance traveled by the particle.

17. (a) Right: _____
   Left: _____
   Stopped: _____

   (b) _____

   (c) _____

18. Find the area of the shaded region analytically.

18. _____

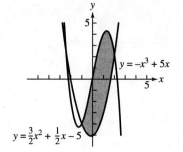

$$y = -x^3 + 5x$$

$$y = \frac{3}{2}x^2 + \frac{1}{2}x - 5$$

19. A curve is given by $y = f(x)$ for $a \leq x \leq b$, where $a > 0$
and $f(x) > 0$. The integral $\int_a^b 2\pi x \cdot f(x)\, dx$
can be used to find which of the following?

    (A) The length of the curve
    (B) The volume of the solid generated by revolving the
        the region below the curve about the x-axis
    (C) The volume of the solid generated by revolving the
        region below the curve about the y-axis
    (D) The area of the surface generated by revolving the
        curve about the x-axis
    (E) The area of the surface generated by revolving the
        curve about the y-axis

19. _____

20. A region is bounded by the line $y = 10 - x$ and the
parabola $y = x^2 - 6x + 10$. Find the volume of the solid
generated by revolving the region about the x-axis.

20. _____

21. Find the length of the curve described by $y = 2x^{3/2}$ for
$0 \leq x \leq 7$.

21. _____

22. A spring has a natural length of 14 cm. A 24-N force
stretches the spring to 17 cm. How much work is done in
stretching the spring from 14 cm to 20 cm?

22. _____

23. Use l'Hôpital's rule to evaluate each limit.

    (a) $\displaystyle \lim_{x \to 4} \frac{x^3 - 3x^2 - 10x + 24}{x^2 - 11x + 28}$

    (b) $\displaystyle \lim_{x \to \infty} \left(1 + \frac{3}{x}\right)^{-2x}$

23. (a) _____

    (b) _____

24. Order the functions from the slowest-growing to
fastest-growing as $x \to \infty$.
$$e^{x/3},\ \ln(5x),\ (x + 2)^3,\ x^4$$

24. _____

25. Evaluate the improper integral $\displaystyle \int_1^5 \frac{dx}{x\sqrt{\ln x}}$ or state
that it diverges.

25. _____

26. Which expression with undetermined coefficients should   26. _____
be used to express $\dfrac{(x+1)^2}{(x-2)^2(x^2-5)}$ as a sum of partial
fractions?

(A) $\dfrac{Ax+B}{(x-2)^2}+\dfrac{Cx+D}{x^2-5}$

(B) $\dfrac{A(x+1)}{x-2}+\dfrac{B(x+1)^2}{(x-2)^2}+\dfrac{(Cx+D)(x+1)^2}{x^2-5}$

(C) $\dfrac{Ax+B}{x-2}+\dfrac{Cx+D}{(x-2)^2}+\dfrac{Ex+F}{x^2-5}$

(D) $\dfrac{A}{x-2}+\dfrac{B}{(x-2)^2}+\dfrac{Cx+D}{x^2-5}$

(E) $\dfrac{A}{x-2}+\dfrac{B}{(x-2)^2}+\dfrac{C}{x-5}+\dfrac{D}{x^2-5}$

27. Evaluate $\displaystyle\int \dfrac{4x^3-x^2+6}{(x+2)(x-3)}\,dx.$ 27. _____

28. Tell whether the series converges or diverges. If it   28. _____
converges, find its sum.

$$4-\dfrac{12}{5}+\dfrac{36}{25}-\dfrac{108}{125}+\cdots+4\left(-\dfrac{3}{5}\right)^n+\cdots$$

29. Find the Maclaurin series for $\dfrac{\ln(1+3x)}{x}.$ 29. _____

30. Let $f(x)=(2x+3)^7.$ Use the Remainder Estimation   30. _____
Theorem to estimate the maximum absolute error when
$f(x)$ is replaced by $2187+10{,}206x$ for $|x|\le 0.06.$

31. Determine the convergence or divergence of the series   31. _____
$\displaystyle\sum_{n=1}^{\infty}\dfrac{(n^2+3)n!}{(2n^2-1)(2n)!}.$ Identify the test (or tests) you use.

32. Which of the following converge conditionally.   32. _____

I. $\displaystyle\sum_{n=1}^{\infty}(-1)^n\dfrac{2\sqrt{n^3+10}}{n+4}$

II. $\displaystyle\sum_{n=1}^{\infty}(-1)^n\dfrac{2}{n}$

III. $\displaystyle\sum_{n=1}^{\infty}(-1)^n\dfrac{3n+5}{(n+1)^3}$

(A) I only   (B) II only   (C) III only
(D) I and III   (E) II and III

33. Find the interval of convergence of the series   33. _____
$\displaystyle\sum_{n=1}^{\infty}\dfrac{(-3)^n(x-2)^n}{\sqrt{n}}$

34. A wheel of radius 4 rolls along the *x*-axis without slipping. The path traced by a point *P* on the wheel's edge is a cycloid. If *P* is initially at the origin, which of the following pairs of equations represents this cycloid?

(A) $x = 4(t - \cos t), y = 4(1 + \sin t)$
(B) $x = 4(t - \sin t), y = 4(1 + \cos t)$
(C) $x = 4(1 - \sin t), y = 4(t - \cos t)$
(D) $x = 4(t - \sin t), y = 4(1 - \cos t)$
(E) $x = 4(1 - \cos t), y = 4(t + \sin t)$

34. _____

35. A semicircle is defined parametrically by $x = 5 - 3 \cos t$, $y = 3 \sin t, \frac{\pi}{6} \le t \le \frac{7\pi}{6}$. Find the area of the surface generated by revolving this curve about the *y*-axis.

35. _____

36. Let $\mathbf{u} = \langle 4, 6 \rangle$ and $\mathbf{v} = \langle -5, 2 \rangle$.

(a) Find $4\mathbf{u} - 3\mathbf{v}$.

(b) Find the magnitude of $\mathbf{v}$.

(c) Find $\mathbf{u} \cdot \mathbf{v}$.

36. (a) _____

(b) _____

(c) _____

37. Solve the initial value problem for $\mathbf{r}$ as a vector function of *t*.

$$\frac{d\mathbf{r}}{dt} = (t + 9)^{1/2}\mathbf{i} + (e^{2t} + 2t)\mathbf{j}, \mathbf{r}(0) = 5\mathbf{i}$$

37. _____

38. A ball is hit at an angle of 42° to the horizontal from 18 feet above the ground. If it hits the ground 22 feet away (in horizontal distance), what was the initial velocity? Assume there is no air resistance.

38. _____

39. (a) Graph the polar curve $r = 2 \sin 5\theta$.

(b) What is the shortest length a θ-interval can have and still produce the graph?

39. (a)

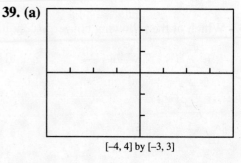

[–4, 4] by [–3, 3]

(b) _____

40. Find the area of the region inside one loop of the lemniscate $r^2 = 18 \sin 2\theta$ and outside the circle $r = 3$.

40. _____

Alternative Assessment

Chapter 1

GROUP ACTIVITY

The only inverse trigonometric functions available on most graphers are $\sin^{-1}$, $\cos^{-1}$, and $\tan^{-1}$. Explain how to calculate inverse secants, inverse cosecants, and inverse cotangents on a grapher.

STUDENT LOG (OR JOURNAL)

Explain why a function that is not one-to-one does not have an inverse function.

DISCUSSION QUESTION

Regression analysis is a useful tool, but predictions made using regression analysis are not always accurate. Describe some of the ways that inaccurate prediction may occur.

Chapter 2

GROUP ACTIVITY

Explain the importance of continuity in discussing limits. Also discuss the value of determining limits as x approaches infinity.

STUDENT LOG (OR JOURNAL)

What complications arise in observing limits with the graphing utility? What of importance is learned by taking limits algebraically?

DISCUSSION QUESTION

In economic problems, the limit of a function can give important information. If a company has an increasing revenue or profit function, what does the limit as x approaches infinity tell us?

Chapter 3

GROUP ACTIVITY

Graph some multiples of e^x and their derivatives. Look at the graphs of e^{nx} for different values of n and their derivatives. What do these graphs show about the simplicity of the natural exponential function?

STUDENT LOG (OR JOURNAL)

Use your graphing utility to graph $y_1 = \ln 2x$, $y_2 = \dfrac{1}{x}$ and $y_3 = \text{NDER } y_1$. What does the graph show about the derivative of y_1 and the chain rule?

DISCUSSION QUESTION

Why is implicit differentiation useful in examining the derivatives of curves that are not functions?

Chapter 4

GROUP ACTIVITY

Sketch the graph of $y = x^3$ and find its antiderivative. Draw some possible antiderivatives. What effect does the constant have?

STUDENT LOG (OR JOURNAL)

Think about the importance of the second derivative test. In economic applications, what does the second derivative test reveal about cost functions and revenue functions?

DISCUSSION QUESTION

Why is it useful to find the linearization of a function? When are linearizations particularly useful?

Chapter 5

GROUP ACTIVITY

Let f be a positive continuous function that is concave up. If the Trapezoidal Rule is used to estimate an area between f and the x-axis, will the result be an overestimate or an underestimate? What if MRAM is used instead?

STUDENT LOG (OR JOURNAL)

In what situations is the definite integral $\int_a^b f(x)\, dx$ of a continuous function f different from the area between the x-axis and the graph of $y = f(x)$, $a \leq x \leq b$?

DISCUSSION QUESTION

Why is it often useful to use a utility such as NINT to evaluate integrals? Why is it important to be able to evaluate integrals analytically?

Chapter 6

GROUP ACTIVITY

In Example 7 on page 337, show that the answer would be the same regardless of Ashley's weight (assuming that her total coasting distance is unchanged).

STUDENT LOG (OR JOURNAL)

What are some guidelines to use when determining u and v for integration by parts?

DISCUSSION QUESTION

Explain why the improved Euler's method is more accurate than the standard Euler's method.

Chapter 7

GROUP ACTIVITY

Think about rotating the same curve about the y-axis and the x-axis. What similarities could be seen about the areas and volumes of these solids? Are they the same?

STUDENT LOG (OR JOURNAL)

What is useful about using integrals to find volumes of solids?

DISCUSSION QUESTION

Discuss the process of finding the center of mass using integrals. (See Exercises 33–35 on page 374.) Of what importance is the center of mass to a moving object?

Chapter 8

GROUP ACTIVITY

A student wrote $\int_{-2}^{2} \dfrac{dx}{x} = \ln|x| \Big]_{-2}^{2} = 0$. Do you agree with this calculation? Discuss.

STUDENT LOG (OR JOURNAL)

What is so important about L'Hôpital's rule and what are some dangers in its use?

DISCUSSION QUESTION

The intensity of a sound in decibels is given by $I = 20 \log \dfrac{P}{k}$, where P is the pressure caused by the sound wave and k is a constant. If P increases by a factor of 10^n, what happens to I? How does this question relate to growth rates of functions?

Chapter 9

GROUP ACTIVITY

Graph the functions cos x and sin x as well as some Taylor polynomials for each. Look at the graphs and determine where the series overestimates and where it underestimates. Test using higher-order polynomials and look at the accuracy change.

STUDENT LOG (OR JOURNAL)

Can the Remainder Estimation Theorem be used to find the *actual* error that occurs when a function f is replaced by a Taylor polynomial? Explain.

DISCUSSION QUESTION

We know the Maclaurin series for ln $(1 + x)$ is $x - \dfrac{x^2}{2} + \dfrac{x^3}{3} - \cdots$. Can you think of a way to derive the series for ln $(1 - x)$ from this?

Chapter 10

GROUP ACTIVITY

Graph in parametric mode $x = n \cos mt$ and $y = n \sin mt$ for different values of m and n and comment on the differences in the graphs. What happens if you switch the sin and cos in the x and y equations?

STUDENT LOG (OR JOURNAL)

Why is graphing in polar coordinates important? Think about cardioids and limaçons as well as conic sections.

DISCUSSION QUESTION

The student is incorrect. $(2\pi, 0)$ and $(-2\pi, -\pi)$ are both equivalent to $(-2\pi, \pi)$, which does satisfy the equation.

Assessment Answers

Chapter 1

Quiz: Sections 1.1–1.3

1. (C)   **2.** (C)

3. (B)   **4.** (D)

5.

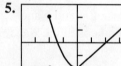

[−4, 4] by [−3, 3]

6. (B)   **7.** (B)

Quiz: Sections 1.4–1.6

1.

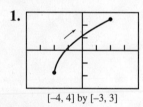

[−4, 4] by [−3, 3]

2. (A)   **3.** (B)

4. (C)   **5.** (B)

6. (E)

Chapter 1 Test Form A

1. (D)

2. (a) $y = \dfrac{3}{5}x - \dfrac{38}{5}$ **(b)** $y = -\dfrac{5}{3}x + 6$

3. (a) $[-3, 3]$ **(b)** $[2, 5]$

    (c) Even

4. (a)

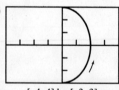

[−4, 4] by [−3, 3]

    (b) $(-\infty, \infty)$ **(c)** $[0, \infty)$

5. (a) $(f \circ g)(x) = \left(\dfrac{1}{x}\right)^2 + 5$ or $\dfrac{1}{x^2} + 5$

    (b) $(g \circ f)(x) = \dfrac{1}{x^2 + 5}$

6. Domain: $(-\infty, \infty)$
    Range: $(^{-}1, \infty)$
    x-intercept: 0
    y-intercept: 0

7. $x \approx 1.262$ **8.** About 2.19 years

9. One possible answer: $x = t, y = t^2 - 4t + 3$,
    $t \le 2$

10. (a)

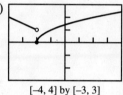

[−4, 4] by [−3, 3]

    (b) $\left(\dfrac{x}{2}\right)^2 + \left(\dfrac{y}{3}\right)^2 = 1$; right half of ellipse

11. (B)

12. $f^{-1}(x) = 3 - x^2, x \ge 0$

13. (a) $y = -20.524 + 19.051 \ln x$
    (b) $x \approx 23.971$ or about 24, in 1999

14. $\dfrac{3\pi}{2}$ ft or about 4.71 ft

15. Period: π; Domain: All reals; Range: $[-1, 5]$

16. $x = \tan^{-1}(0.25) \approx 0.245$,
    $x = \pi + \tan^{-1}(0.25) \approx 3.387$

Chapter 1 Test Form B

1. (C)

2. (a) $y = -\dfrac{4}{3}x + 5$ (b) $y = \dfrac{3}{4}x - \dfrac{55}{4}$

3. (a) $(-\infty, -5] \cup [5, \infty)$

   (b) $[-2, \infty)$ (c) Even

4. (a)

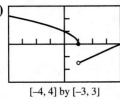

[-4, 4] by [-3, 3]

   (b) $(-\infty, \infty)$ (c) $(-1.5, \infty)$

5. (a) $(f \circ g)(x) = \dfrac{1}{5x^2 - 2}$

   (b) $(g \circ f)(x) = \dfrac{5}{(x-2)^2}$

6. Domain: $(-\infty, \infty)$

Range: $(-\infty, 9)$

x-intercept: 2

y-intercept: 8

7. $x \approx -2.585$ **8.** About 2.41 years

9. One possible answer: $x = t, y = t^2 + 6t - 7$, $t \geq -3$

10. (a)

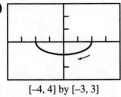

[-4, 4] by [-3, 3]

   (b) $\left(\dfrac{x}{2}\right)^2 + y^2 = 1$; lower half of ellipse

11. (C)

12. $f^{-1}(x) = x^2 - 5, x \leq 0$

13. (a) $y \approx -20.907 + 30.827 \ln x$

   (b) $x \approx 31.05$ or about 31, in 2006

14. $\dfrac{35\pi}{6}$ m or about 18.33 m

15. Period: π; Domain: $x \neq k\pi$ for integers k; Range: All reals

16. $x = \cos^{-1}\left(-\dfrac{1}{3}\right) \approx 1.911$,

$x = 2\pi - \cos^{-1}\left(-\dfrac{1}{3}\right) \approx 4.373$

Chapter 2

Quiz: Sections 2.1–2.2

1. (C)   **2.** (C)

3. (D)   **4.** (B)

5. (E)   **6.** (D)

7. (B)   **8.** (A)

Quiz: Sections 2.3–2.4

1. (C)   **2.** (D)

3. One possible answer:

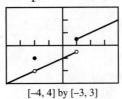

[-4, 4] by [-3, 3]

4. (B)   **5.** (A)

6. (E)   **7.** (D)

Chapter 2 Test Form A

1. (a) 1   (b) -2

   (c) Does not exist, because the left- and right-hand limits are different.

   (d) 1

2. 10   **3.** (E)

4. 3; $3 - x^2 \leq 3 + x^2 \sin\dfrac{1}{x} \leq 3 + x^2$ and

$\lim_{x \to 0} (3 - x^2) = \lim_{x \to 0} (3 + x^2) = 3$,

so $\lim_{x \to 0}\left(3 + x^2 \sin\dfrac{1}{x}\right) = 3$.

5. (a) $\dfrac{2}{3}$ (b) $-\dfrac{2}{3}$

   (c) $y = \dfrac{2}{3}, y = -\dfrac{2}{3}$

6. (C)

7. (a) $x = -4, x = 4$

   (b) Left-hand limits at -4 and 4 are ∞. Right-hand limits at -4 and 4 are $-\infty$.

8. (a) e^x (b) $-2x^3$

9. Removable discontinuity at $x = -2$; infinite discontinuity at $x = -3$.

10. $a = -\dfrac{1}{4}$

11. One possible answer:

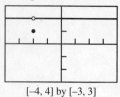

[−4, 4] by [−3, 3]

12. Because h is a composite of two continuous functions: $h(x) = (g \circ f)(x)$, where $f(x) = x^2 - 4x - 6$ and $g(x) = |x|$.

13. 17

14. (a) 20   **(b)** $y = 20x - 20$

    (c) $y = -0.05x + 20.1$

15. 45.6 m/sec

Chapter 2 Test Form B

1. (a) 2   **(b)** −1

    (c) Does not exist, because the left- and right-hand limits are different.

    (d) −1

2. −57   **3.** (A)

4. 5; $5 - x^2 \leq 5 - x^2 \cos \dfrac{1}{x} \leq 5 + x^2$

    and $\lim\limits_{x \to 0} (5 - x^2) = \lim\limits_{x \to 0} (5 + x^2) = 5$,

    so $\lim\limits_{x \to 0} \left(5 - x^2 \cos \dfrac{1}{x}\right) = 5$.

5. (a) $-\dfrac{5}{4}$ **(b)** $\dfrac{5}{4}$

    (c) $y = -\dfrac{5}{4}, y = \dfrac{5}{4}$

6. (C)

7. (a) $x = -4, x = 2$

    (b) Left-hand limits at −4 and 2 are −∞. Right-hand limits at −4 and 2 are ∞.

8. (a) $3x^2$ **(b)** 7^{-x}

9. Removable discontinuity at $x = -3$; infinite discontinuity at $x = 3$.

10. $m = 2$

11. One possible answer:

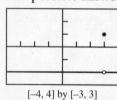

[−4, 4] by [−3, 3]

12. Because h is a composite of two continuous functions: $h(x) = (g \circ f)(x)$, where $f(x) = x^5 + 2x - 3$ and $g(x) = \sin x$.

13. −5

14. (a) 24   **(b)** $y = 24x - 48$

    (c) $y = -\dfrac{1}{24}x + 48\dfrac{1}{6}$

15. 254.4 in./sec

Chapter 3

Quiz: Sections 3.1–3.3

1. (D)

2.

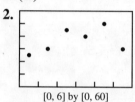

[0, 6] by [0, 60]

3. (E)   **4.** (C)

5. (C)   **6.** (B)

Quiz: Sections 3.4–3.6

1.

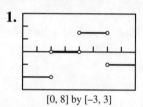

[0, 8] by [−3, 3]

2. (B)   **3.** (A)

4. (A)   **5.** (D)

6. (E)   **7.** (A)

Quiz: Sections 3.7–3.9

1. (B)   **2.** (D)

3. (E)   **4.** (A)

5. (A)   **6.** (C)

7. (D)

Chapter 3 Test Form A

1. $f'(2) = \lim\limits_{h \to 0} \dfrac{[(2 + h)^2 - 3] - (2^2 - 3)}{h} = 4$

2.

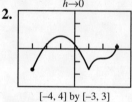

[−4, 4] by [−3, 3]

3. (D)

4. (a) 500

    (b) No, $f'(3)$ does not exist. Also, $f'(x)$ is zero for all x where $f'(x)$ is defined.

5. (a) $12x^3 - 27x^2 + 5$;

(b) $36x^2 - 54x$

6. (a) -12 (b) 360

7. (a) 3 ft   (b) 1 ft/sec

(c) 19 ft/sec   (d) 18 ft/sec^2

(e) $t = \sqrt{\dfrac{8}{3}} \approx 1.633$ sec

8. (a)

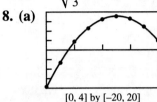

[0, 4] by [–20, 20]

(b) 18 ft/sec; 0 ft/sec; -12 ft/sec

9. $\dfrac{-\sin x - \sin x \tan x - \sec x}{(1 + \tan x)^2}$

10. $\left(\dfrac{\pi}{6}, \dfrac{2}{\sqrt{3}}\right), \left(\dfrac{5\pi}{6}, -\dfrac{2}{\sqrt{3}}\right)$

11. $2x \cos(x^2 - 1)$ **12.** $y = 72x - 180$

13. (B)   **14.** $-\dfrac{2x + 5y}{5x + 5y^4}$

15. $\dfrac{-2}{4x^2 + 1}$ **16.** $-4^{-x+3} \ln 4$

17. (B)

Chapter 3 Test Form B

1. $f'(5) = \lim\limits_{h \to 5} \dfrac{[(5 + h)^2 + (5 + h)] - (5^2 + 5)}{h} = 11$

2.

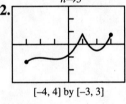

[–4, 4] by [–3, 3]

3. (B)

4. (a) 100

(b) No, since there is a vertical tangent at $x = 2$ and $f'(2)$ does not exist.

5. (a) $21x^2 + 8x - 6$ (b) $42x + 8$

6. (a) -198 (b) $-\dfrac{19}{27}$

7. (a) 225 ft   (b) 45 ft/sec

(c) 145 ft/sec   (d) 60 ft/sec^2

(e) $t = \sqrt{\dfrac{5}{6}} \approx 0.913$ sec

8. (a)

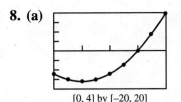

[0, 4] by [–20, 20]

(b) 0 ft/sec; 12 ft/sec; 20 ft/sec

9. $\dfrac{\sec^2 x + \sin x \sec^2 x - \sin x}{(1 + \sin x)^2}$

10. $\left(\dfrac{\pi}{3}, \sqrt{3}\right), \left(\dfrac{2\pi}{3}, -\sqrt{3}\right) \left(\dfrac{4\pi}{3}, \sqrt{3}\right), \left(\dfrac{5\pi}{3}, -\sqrt{3}\right)$

11. $-15x^2 \sin 5x^3$ **12.** $y = \dfrac{1}{3}x + 16$

13. (E)   **14.** $\dfrac{3x^2 + 4y^2}{4y^3 - 8xy}$

15. $\dfrac{3}{\sqrt{1 - 9x^2}}$ **16.** $2 \cdot 3^{2x+5} \ln 3$

17. (C)

Chapter 4

Quiz: Sections 4.1–4.3

1. (D)   **2.** (B)

3. (A)   **4.** (E)

5. (D)   **6.** (D)

7. (B)

Quiz: Sections 4.4–4.6

1. (C)   **2.** (B)

3. (B)   **4.** (E)

5. (C)   **6.** (D)

7. (A)

Chapter 4 Test Form A

1. (a) Min: -2, at $x = 2$

     Max: 2, at $x = 0$

(b) $(-\infty, 0) \cup (2, \infty)$ (c) $(0, 2)$

(d) $(1, \infty)$ (e) $(-\infty, 1)$

2. (a) $[-6, 0], [6, \infty)$ (b) $(-\infty, -6], [0, 6]$

(c) $(-\infty, -\sqrt{12}), (\sqrt{12}, \infty)$

(d) $(-\sqrt{12}, \sqrt{12})$

(e) Min: -1313 at $x = \pm 6$

     Max: -17 at $x = 0$

(f) $(-\sqrt{12}, -737), (\sqrt{12}, -737)$

3. (a) $[-1.327, 1.114]$

   (b) $(-\infty, -1.327], [1.114, \infty)$

   (c) $(-2.283, -0.233), (2.095, \infty)$

   (d) $(-\infty, -2.283), (-0.233, 2.095)$

   (e) Min: -0.926 at $x = -1.327$
       Max: 0.520 at $x = 1.114$

   (f) $(-2.283, -0.684), (-0.233, -0.245),$
       $(2.095, 0.384)$

4. (a) None   (b) -3

   (c) $-\dfrac{5}{3}, 1$

5. $g(x) = 2x^2 + x - 52$

6. (a) About 7.705 cm by 9.705 cm by 2.148 cm

   (b) About 160.584 cm^3

7. (a) Possible answers:
       Increasing: $-4 \le x \le -1.5, 2 \le x \le 4$
       Decreasing: $-1.5 \le x \le 2$
       Local min: $x \approx 2$
       Local max: $x \approx -1.5$

   (b) $f'(x) = 4.919x^2 - 2.550x - 14.126$

   (c) $f(x) = 1.640x^3 - 1.275x^2 - 14.126x$

8. (a) $a = -6$ (b) $a = -18$

9. (C)

10. $L(x) = \dfrac{7}{2}x - \dfrac{3}{2}$ 11. $x \approx 1.830934$

12. (a) $dy = \dfrac{5}{5x - 2}dx$ (b) $dy \approx 0.01875$

13. $\dfrac{25}{648} \approx 0.039$ ft/min

14. $-\dfrac{180}{\sqrt{13}} \approx -49.9$ ft/sec

Chapter 4 Test Form B

1. (a) Min: -2 at $x = -2$
       Max: 2 at $x = 0$

   (b) $(-2, 0)$ (c) $(-\infty, -2) \cup (0, \infty)$

   (d) $(-\infty, -1)$ (e) $(-1, \infty)$

2. (a) $(-\infty, -3], [0, 3]$ (b) $[-3, 0], [3, \infty)$

   (c) $(-\sqrt{3}, \sqrt{3})$ (d) $(-\infty, -\sqrt{3}), (\sqrt{3}, \infty)$

   (e) Min: 11 at $x = 0$
       Max: 92 at $x = \pm 3$

   (f) $(-\sqrt{3}, 56), (\sqrt{3}, 56)$

3. (a) $(-\infty, 0.106], [1.894, \infty)$

   (b) $[0.106, 1.894]$

   (c) $(-\infty, -0.175), (0.355, \infty)$

   (d) $(-0.175, 0.355)$

   (e) Min: 0.351 at $x \approx 1.894$
       Max: 1.053 at $x \approx 0.106$

   (f) $(-0.175, 0.727), (0.355, 0.875)$

4. (a) None   (b) 4

   (c) $-2, 2$

5. $g(x) = 2x^3 - 47$

6. (a) About 5.873 cm by 13.873 cm by 2.063 cm

   (b) About 168.126 cm^3

7. (a) Possible answers:
       Increasing: $-2.5 \le x \le 3$
       Decreasing: $-4 \le x \le -2.5, 3 \le x \le 4$
       Local min: $x \approx -2.5$
       Local max: $x \approx 3$

   (b) $f'(x) = -4.869x^2 + 2.850x + 31.238$

   (c) $f(x) = -1.623x^3 + 1.425x^2 + 31.238x$

8. (a) $a = -50$ (b) $a = -24$

9. (B)   10. $L(x) = \dfrac{31}{4}x - 14$

11. $x \approx 2.506921$

12. (a) $dy = 3e^{3x-5}dx$ (b) $dy \approx 0.326$

13. $-\dfrac{432}{625\pi} \approx -0.220$ ft^3/min

14. $\dfrac{145}{\sqrt{13}} \approx 40.2$ ft/sec

Chapter 5

Quiz: Sections 5.1–5.3

1. (E)

2.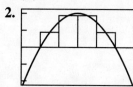

   $[0, 6]$ by $[-2.25, 2.25]$

3. (D)   4. (B)

5. (C)   6. (C)

7. (A)

Quiz: Sections 5.4–5.5

1. (B)   2. (C)

3. (B)   4. (D)

5. (D)   6. (C)

7. (D)

Chapter 5 Test Form A

1. (a) ≈ 36.92 (b) 37.29

2. ≈ 30.928 3. $\dfrac{3}{2}(a^4 - a^2)$

4. ≈ 216.128 5. (B)

6. 40 7. 1

8. (a)

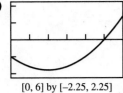

[0, 6] by [–2.25, 2.25]

(b) −6 **(c)** $\dfrac{22}{3}$

9. (a) −4 **(b)** $4 - 3x$

10. (a) 0 cm **(b)** 5.25 cm

 (c) −2 cm/sec **(d)** At $t = 5$ sec

 (e) At $t \approx 3.5$ sec

11. 0.75 **12.** 38,400 ft^2

Chapter 5 Test Form B

1. (a) ≈ 67.00 **(b)** 67.66

2. ≈ 58.769 **3.** $\dfrac{5}{2}(b^2 - a^4)$

4. ≈ 1.098 **5.** (C)

6. −145 **7.** $1 - \dfrac{1}{\sqrt{3}} \approx 0.423$

8. (a)

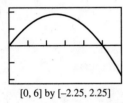

[0, 6] by [–2.25, 2.25]

(b) 5.4 **(c)** 7.1

9. (a) −102 **(b)** $3x + 2$

10. (a) 0 ft **(b)** −1.5 ft

 (c) 3 ft/sec **(d)** At $t = 4$ sec

 (e) At $t = 2$ sec

11. −26 **12.** 30,280 cm^2

Semester Test

Semester Test Chapters 1–4 Form A

1. (a) $y = \dfrac{4}{5}x - 7$ **(b)** $y = -\dfrac{5}{4}x + \dfrac{13}{4}$

2. (a)

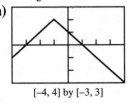

[–4, 4] by [–3, 3]

(b) All reals **(c)** $(-\infty, 2]$

3. (B) **4.** ≈ 19.525 years

5. (a)

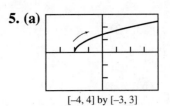

[–4, 4] by [–3, 3]

(b) One possible answer:

 $y = \sqrt{x} + 2$; entire curve

6. One possible answer:

 $x = 13 - 6t,\ y = 5 + 3t,\ 0 \le t \le 1$

7. $f^{-1}(x) = -\ln\left(\dfrac{20}{3x} - \dfrac{1}{3}\right)$

8. $x = \dfrac{\ln 5}{\ln 1.08} \approx 20.91$

9. (a) $\dfrac{2\pi}{3}$

 (b) $x \ne \dfrac{\pi}{6} + \dfrac{k\pi}{3}$ for integers k

 (c) $(-\infty, -1] \cup [3, \infty)$

 (d)

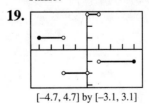

[–π, π] by [–5, 5]

10. $x = \sin^{-1}(0.2) \approx 0.201$,

 $x = \pi - \sin^{-1} 0.2 \approx 2.940$

11. (B) **12.** $\dfrac{9}{2}$

13. (a) $-\infty$ **(b)** 1

 (c) ∞ **(d)** 1

14. $\dfrac{3}{2}x^3$

15. $x = -4$ (infinite discontinuity),

 $x = 4$ (jump discontinuity)

16. $g(x) = \dfrac{x + 4}{x - 3}$

17. (a) −48 ft/sec **(b)** −64 ft/sec

18. No; left- and right-hand derivatives are not the same.

19.

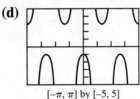

[–4.7, 4.7] by [–3.1, 3.1]

20.

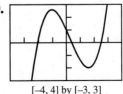

[–4, 4] by [–3, 3]

21. $\left(0, \dfrac{2}{5}\right) \cup \left(\dfrac{2}{5}, \infty\right)$ **22.** (B)

23. $\dfrac{x^2 - 2x - 14}{(x-1)^2}$

24. (a) $4x^3 - 15x^2 + 9$ (b) $12x^2 - 30x$

25. (a) 242.5 m (b) 48.5 m/min

(c) 148.5 m/min (d) 60 m/min^2

(e) $t = 0.5$ min

26. (a)

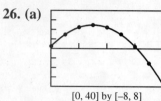

[0, 40] by [−8, 8]

(b) $t = 10$: ≈ 0.2 ft/sec
$t = 25$: ≈ -0.4 ft/sec

27. (a)

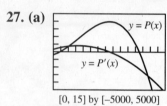

[0, 15] by [−5000, 5000]

(b) \$480.00 (c) \$1711.11

(d) \$3920.00

28. $\dfrac{12 \sec^2 x - 3 \sec x - 3 \tan x \sin x}{(4 - \cos x)^2}$

29. $6x \sec(3x^2) \tan(3x^2)$ **30.** 81

31. $y = \sqrt{3}x - 2$ **32.** $\dfrac{4x + y \sin xy}{3 - x \sin xy}$

33. $\dfrac{1}{1 + (x - 4)^2}$ **34.** (B)

35. $2e^{2x} - \dfrac{2}{x}$

36. Min: 1 at $x = 0$
Max: 3 at $x = 1$

37. (a) $[0, \infty)$ (b) $(-\infty, 0]$

(c) $\left(-\infty, \dfrac{1}{3}\right), (1, \infty)$ (d) $\left(\dfrac{1}{3}, 1\right)$

(e) Min: -3 at $x = 0$
Max: None

(f) $\left(\dfrac{1}{3}, -\dfrac{961}{324}\right), \left(1, -\dfrac{35}{12}\right)$

38. (D)

39. $f(x) = \dfrac{4x^3}{3} - 3x - \cos x + C$

40.

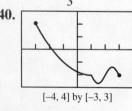

[−4, 4] by [−3, 3]

41. (a) $V(x) = \left(\dfrac{35 - 2x}{2}\right)(22 - 2x)(x)$
$= 2x^3 - 57x^2 + 385x$

(b) Domain: (0, 11)

(c) Volume ≈ 760.850 in^3 at $x \approx 4.393$

42. $a = 3; b = -45$

Semester Test Chapters 1–4 Form B

1. (a) $y = -\dfrac{3}{4}x + \dfrac{5}{2}$ (b) $y = \dfrac{4}{3}x - 10$

2. (a)

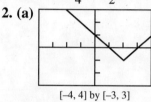

[−4, 4] by [−3, 3]

(b) All reals (c) $[-1, \infty)$

3. (D) **4.** ≈ 26.384 years

5. (a)

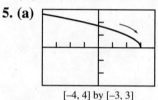

[−4, 4] by [−3, 3]

(b) One possible answer:
$y = \sqrt{3 - x}$; entire curve

6. One possible answer:
$x = 4 + 5t, y = 11 - 8t, 0 \le t \le 1$

7. $f^{-1}(x) = -\ln\left(\dfrac{3}{x} - \dfrac{2}{5}\right)$

8. $x = \dfrac{\ln 4}{\ln 1.06} \approx 23.79$

9. (a) π

(b) $x \ne \dfrac{k\pi}{2}$ for integers k

(c) $(-\infty, -4] \cup [1, \infty)$

(d)

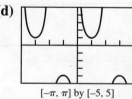

[$-\pi, \pi$] by [−5, 5]

10. $x = \cos^{-1}(0.6) \approx 0.927$,
$x = 2\pi - \cos^{-1}(0.6) \approx 5.356$

11. (E) **12.** $-\dfrac{14}{5}$

13. (a) 2 (b) $-\infty$

(c) -1 (d) ∞

14. $\dfrac{5}{3}x^2$

15. $x = -2$ (infinite discontinuity)

16. $g(x) = \dfrac{x-1}{x+5}$

17. (a) -64 ft/sec   **(b)** -96 ft/sec

18. No; function is discontinuous.

19.

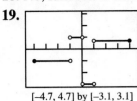

[−4.7, 4.7] by [−3.1, 3.1]

20.

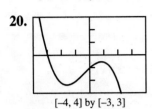

[−4, 4] by [−3, 3]

21. $\left(-\dfrac{4}{3}, 0\right) \cup (0, \infty)$

22. (D)

23. $\dfrac{x^2 + 8x + 10}{(x+4)^2}$

24. (a) $5x^4 + 24x^2 - 4x$ **(b)** $20x^3 + 48x - 4$

25. (a) -28 m   **(b)** -7 m/min

    (c) -35 m/min   **(d)** -22 m/min^2

    (e) $t = \dfrac{5}{3}$ min

26. (a)

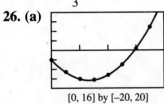

[0, 16] by [−20, 20]

    (b) $t = 2$: ≈ -2.5 ft/sec

        $t = 12$: ≈ 5 ft/sec

27. (a)

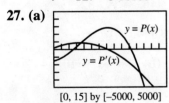

[0, 15] by [−5000, 5000]

    (b) $840.00   **(c)** $648.15

    (d) $2840.00

28. $\dfrac{10 \cos x - 2 + 2\tan^2 x}{(5 - \sec x)^2}$

29. $12x^2 \sec^2(4x^3)$ **30.** 64

31. $y = -2x + \dfrac{3\sqrt{3}}{2}$ **32.** $-\dfrac{5 - y\cos xy}{6y - x\cos xy}$

33. $\dfrac{1}{|x+3|\sqrt{(x+3)^2 - 1}}$ **34.** (D)

35. $\dfrac{1}{x} - 2x\,e^{x^2}$

36. Min: -1 at $x = 2$

    Max: 2 at $x = -1$

37. (a) $(-\infty, 1]$ **(b)** $[1, \infty)$

    (c) $\left(-\dfrac{2}{3}, 0\right)$ **(d)** $\left(-\infty, -\dfrac{2}{3}\right), (0, \infty)$

    (e) Min: None

        Max: $\dfrac{17}{12}$ at $x = 1$

    (f) $\left(-\dfrac{2}{3}, -\dfrac{104}{81}\right), (0, 0)$

38. (E)

39. $f(x) = \dfrac{5x^2}{2} + 4x - \sin x + C$

40.

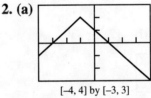

[−4, 4] by [−3, 3]

41. (a) $V(x) = \left(\dfrac{36 - 2x}{2}\right)(20 - 2x)(x)$

            $= 2x^3 - 56x^2 + 360x$

    (b) Domain: (0, 10)

    (c) Volume ≈ 672.504 in^3 at $x \approx 4.127$

42. $a = -2; b = 30$

Semester Test Chapters 1–5 Form A

1. (a) $y = \dfrac{4}{5}x - 7$ **(b)** $y = -\dfrac{5}{4}x + \dfrac{13}{4}$

2. (a)

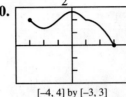

[−4, 4] by [−3, 3]

    (b) All reals   **(c)** $(-\infty, 2]$

3. (B)   **4.** ≈ 19.525 years

5. (a)

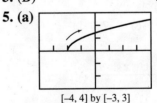

[−4, 4] by [−3, 3]

    (b) One possible answer:

        $y = \sqrt{x} + 2$; entire curve

6. One possible answer:

    $x = 13 - 6t,\ y = 5 + 3t,\ 0 \le t \le 1$

7. $f^{-1}(x) = -\ln\left(\dfrac{20}{3x} - \dfrac{1}{3}\right)$

8. (a) $\dfrac{2\pi}{3}$

    (b) $x \neq \dfrac{k\pi}{6} + \dfrac{\pi}{3}$ for integers k

    (c) $(-\infty, -1] \cup [3, \infty)$

(d)

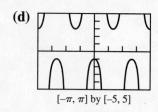

$[-\pi, \pi]$ by $[-5, 5]$

9. $x = \sin^{-1}(0.2) \approx 0.201$,

$x = \pi - \sin^{-1} 0.2 \approx 2.940$

10. (B)   **11.** $\dfrac{9}{2}$

12. (a) $-\infty$ **(b)** 1

(c) ∞ **(d)** 1

13. $g(x) = \dfrac{x + 4}{x - 3}$

14. (a) -48 ft/sec   **(b)** -64 ft/sec

15. No; left- and right-hand derivatives are not the same.

16.

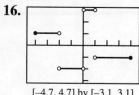

$[-4.7, 4.7]$ by $[-3.1, 3.1]$

17. $\left(0, \dfrac{2}{5}\right) \cup \left(\dfrac{2}{5}, \infty\right)$ **18.** (B)

19. $\dfrac{x^2 - 2x - 14}{(x - 1)^2}$

20. (a) $4x^3 - 15x^2 + 9$ **(b)** $12x^2 - 30x$

21. (a)

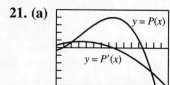

$[0, 15]$ by $[-5000, 5000]$

(b) \$480.00   **(c)** \$1711.11

(d) \$3920.00

22. $\dfrac{12 \sec^2 x - 3 \sec x - 3 \tan x \sin x}{(4 - \cos x)^2}$

23. $6x \sec (3x^2) \tan (3x^2)$ **24.** 81

25. $y = \sqrt{3}x - 2$ **26.** $\dfrac{4x + y \sin xy}{3 - x \sin xy}$

27. $\dfrac{1}{1 + (x - 4)^2}$ **28.** (B)

29. $2e^{2x} - \dfrac{2}{x}$

30. Min: 1 at $x = 0$

Max: 3 at $x = 1$

31. (a) $[0, \infty)$ **(b)** $(-\infty, 0]$

(c) $\left(-\infty, \dfrac{1}{3}\right), (1, \infty)$ **(d)** $\left(\dfrac{1}{3}, 1\right)$

(e) Min: -3 at $x = 0$

Max: None

(f) $\left(\dfrac{1}{3}, -\dfrac{961}{324}\right), \left(1, -\dfrac{35}{12}\right)$

32. (D)

33. $f(x) = \dfrac{4x^3}{3} - 3x - \cos x + C$

34.

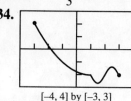

$[-4, 4]$ by $[-3, 3]$

35. (a) $V(x) = \left(\dfrac{35 - 2x}{2}\right)(22 - 2x)(x)$

$= 2x^3 - 57x^2 + 385x$

(b) Domain: $(0, 11)$

(c) Volume ≈ 760.850 in^3 at $x \approx 4.393$

36. (E)   **37.** $x_2 \approx 19.379$

38. (a) -80 ft^3/sec   **(b)** -4 ft^2/sec

(c) $\dfrac{25}{3\sqrt{21}} \approx 1.818$ ft/sec

39. 180 ft

40. $\displaystyle\int_7^{15} \left(2x + \dfrac{1}{x^2}\right) dx$

41. (a) 7   **(b)** 5

(c) -5

42. $\dfrac{3\pi}{4} + 2$ **43.** ≈ 7.498

44. (a) -4 **(b)** $\dfrac{508}{7}$

(c) -1

45. (D)   **46.** ≈ 19.482

Semester Test Chapters 1–5 Form B

1. (a) $y = -\dfrac{3}{4}x + \dfrac{5}{2}$ **(b)** $y = \dfrac{4}{3}x - 10$

2. (a)

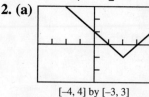

$[-4, 4]$ by $[-3, 3]$

(b) All reals   **(c)** $[-1, \infty)$

3. (D)   **4.** ≈ 26.384 years

5. (a)

$[-4, 4]$ by $[-3, 3]$

(b) One possible answer:

$y = \sqrt{3} - x$;

entire curve

6. One possible answer:
$x = 4 + 5t, y = 11 - 8t, 0 \le t \le 1$

7. $f^{-1}(x) = -\ln\left(\dfrac{3}{x} - \dfrac{2}{5}\right)$

8. (a) π

   (b) $x \ne \dfrac{k\pi}{2}$ for integers k

   (c) $(-\infty, -4] \cup [1, \infty)$

   (d)

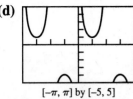

[−π, π] by [−5, 5]

9. $x = \cos^{-1}(0.6) \approx 0.927,$
   $x = 2\pi - \cos^{-1}(0.6) \approx 5.356$

10. (E)   **11.** $-\dfrac{14}{5}$

12. (a) 2   **(b)** $-\infty$

   (c) -1 **(d)** ∞

13. $g(x) = \dfrac{x - 1}{x + 5}$

14. (a) -64 ft/sec   **(b)** -96 ft/sec

15. No; function is discontinuous.

16.

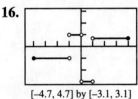

[−4.7, 4.7] by [−3.1, 3.1]

17. $\left(-\dfrac{4}{3}, 0\right) \cup (0, \infty)$

18. (D)   **19.** $\dfrac{x^2 + 8x + 10}{(x + 4)^2}$

20. (a) $5x^4 + 24x^2 - 4x$ **(b)** $20x^3 + 48x - 4$

21. (a)

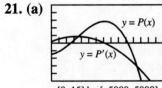

[0, 15] by [−5000, 5000]

   (b) \$840.00   **(c)** \$648.15

   (d) \$2840.00

22. $\dfrac{10\cos x - 2 + 2\tan^2 x}{(5 - \sec x)^2}$

23. $12x^2 \sec^2(4x^3)$ **24.** 64

25. $y = -2x + \dfrac{3\sqrt{3}}{2}$ **26.** $-\dfrac{5 - y\cos xy}{6y - x\cos xy}$

27. $\dfrac{1}{|x + 3|\sqrt{(x + 3)^2 - 1}}$ **28.** (D)

29. $\dfrac{1}{x} - 2x\, e^{x^2}$

30. Min: -1 at $x = 2$
   Max: 2 at $x = -1$

31. (a) $(-\infty, 1]$ **(b)** $[1, \infty)$

   (c) $\left(-\dfrac{2}{3}, 0\right)$ **(d)** $\left(-\infty, -\dfrac{2}{3}\right), (0, \infty)$

   (e) Min: None

      Max: $\dfrac{17}{12}$ at $x = 1$

   (f) $\left(-\dfrac{2}{3}, -\dfrac{104}{81}\right), (0, 0)$

32. (E)

33. $f(x) = \dfrac{5x^2}{2} + 4x - \sin x + C$

34.

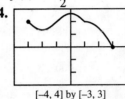

[−4, 4] by [−3, 3]

35. (a) $V(x) = \left(\dfrac{36 - 2x}{2}\right)(20 - 2x)(x)$
      $= 2x^3 - 56x^2 + 360x$

   (b) Domain: $(0, 10)$

   (c) Volume ≈ 672.504 in^3 at $x \approx 4.127$

36. (B)   **37.** $x_2 \approx 0.736$

38. (a) -243 ft^3/sec   **(b)** -108 ft^2/sec

   (c) $-\dfrac{6}{\sqrt{146}} \approx -0.497$ ft/sec

39. 930 ft

40. $\displaystyle\int_3^{11}\left(5x^2 - \dfrac{3}{x}\right) dx$

41. (a) -4 **(b)** -1

   (c) -67

42. $5 - \pi$ **43.** ≈ 4.985

44. (a) 186   **(b)** $\dfrac{93}{5}$

   (c) $\dfrac{2}{\sqrt{3}} \approx 1.155$

45. (E)   **46.** ≈ 10.783

Chapter 6

Quiz: Sections 6.1–6.3

1. (B)

2. $y = x^3 - 2x + 1$

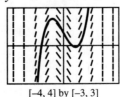

[−4, 4] by [−3, 3]

3. (C)   **4.** (C)

5. (D)   **6.** (A)

Quiz: Sections 6.4–6.6

1. (D)   **2.** (C)

3. (D)   **4.** (B)

5. (D)

6.

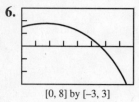

[0, 8] by [–3, 3]

Chapter 6 Test Form A

1. (D)   **2.** $\frac{1}{3}e^{3x} - 4\sin x + C$

3. $y = \frac{5}{3}x^3 - 7x - 12$

4.

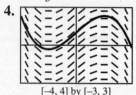

[–4, 4] by [–3, 3]

5. $\frac{1}{6}(\ln x)^6 + C$ **6.** $e - 1$

7. $y = \sqrt[3]{\sin x + 125}$

8. $x\cos^{-1} 2x - \frac{1}{2}\sqrt{1 - 4x^2} + C$

9. $(4x^2 - 11x + 11)e^x + C$

10. $t\sin(\ln t) + t\cos(\ln t) + C$

11. (a) 0.578 year   **(b)** 3.260 years

12. (a) 300 m   **(b)** 20.8 sec

13. (a) $\frac{dP}{dt} = 0.031P$ **(b)** $P = 56{,}800\, e^{0.031t}$

14. (a) $k = 0.08$; carrying capacity = 2000

(b) $P = \dfrac{2000}{1 + 199e^{-0.08t}}$

(c) 46.8 years

15. (D)

16.

x	y
2.0	3.500
2.1	2.158
2.2	1.530
2.3	1.264
2.4	1.183
2.5	1.201
2.6	1.274
2.7	1.381
2.8	1.513
2.9	1.665
3.0	1.837

Chapter 6 Test Form B

1. (A)   **2.** $\frac{1}{3}\sin 3x - 5e^x + C$

3. $y = 2x^4 + 5x - 35$

4.

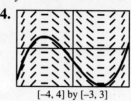

[–4, 4] by [–3, 3]

5. $\frac{1}{4}e^{x^4 + 2x^2} + C$ **6.** -1

7. $y = \tan^{-1}(x^2 - 9)$

8. $x\cot^{-1} 3x + \frac{1}{6}\ln(1 + 9x^2) + C$

9. $\frac{1}{13}(3\sin 2x - 2\cos 2x)e^{3x} + C$

10. $(t^4 - 2t^2 + 2)e^{t^2} + C$

11. (a) 0.433 year   **(b)** 2.012 years

12. (a) 2000 m   **(b)** 87.1 sec

13. (a) $\frac{dP}{dt} = 0.047P$

(b) $P = 83{,}400\, e^{0.047t}$

14. (a) $k = 0.06$; carrying capacity = 800

(b) $P = \dfrac{800}{1 + 31e^{-0.06t}}$

(c) 61.4 years

15. (C)

16.

x	y
1.0	2.500
1.1	2.042
1.2	1.840
1.3	1.754
1.4	1.732
1.5	1.749
1.6	1.787
1.7	1.837
1.8	1.892
1.9	1.949
2.0	2.006

Chapter 7

Quiz: Sections 7.1–7.3

1. (C)   **2.** (A)

3. (D)   **4.** (B)

5. (A)   **6.** (C)

7. (B)

Chapter 8

Quiz: Sections 7.4–7.5

1. (E)	**2.** (E)
3. (B)	**4.** (E)
5. (D)	**6.** (D)

Chapter 7 Test Form A

1. (a) Right: $t > 2$; left: $0 \leq t < 2$; stopped: $t = 2$

    (b) $\dfrac{65}{3}$ m   **(c)** $\dfrac{97}{3}$ m

2. (a) At $x = -4$ m   **(b)** 13 m

3. About \$2183 billion   **4.** $\dfrac{96}{5}$

5. $\dfrac{500}{3}$ **6.** (C)

7. $\left(\dfrac{189}{5} + 36 \ln \dfrac{2}{5}\right)\pi \approx 15.122$

8. $\dfrac{13\pi}{3}$ **9.** $\dfrac{61\pi}{432}$

10. $\dfrac{27}{2}$ **11.** (E)

12. 40   **13.** 48 in.-lb

14. About 488,580 ft-lb

15. (a) About 16% (using 68-95-99.7 rule)
     or 15.9% (uing NINT)

    (b) About 51.7%   **(c)** About 233 fish

Chapter 7 Test Form B

1. (a) Right: $0 \leq t < 3$; left: $t > 3$; stopped: $t = 3$

    (b) -18 m   **(c)** 54 m

2. (a) At $x = 3$ m   **(b)** $\dfrac{19}{2}$ m

3. About \$1351 billion   **4.** $\dfrac{448}{15}$

5. $\dfrac{256}{3}$ **6.** (B)

7. $(15 - 8 \ln 4)\pi \approx 12.283$

8. $\dfrac{52\pi}{3}$ **9.** $\dfrac{98\pi}{81}$

10. 48   **11.** (A)

12. 48   **13.** 150 in.-lb

14. About 24,127 ft-lb

15. (a) About 2.5% (using 68-95-99.7 rule)
     or 2.3% (using NINT)

    (b) About 33.4%   **(c)** About 158 snakes

Chapter 8

Quiz: Sections 8.1–8.2

1. (C)	**2.** (D)
3. (C)	**4.** (B)
5. (B)	**6.** (C)
7. (B)	**8.** (C)

Quiz: Sections 8.3–8.4

1. (D)	**2.** (A)
3. (B)	**4.** (C)
5. (D)	**6.** (D)
7. (A)	

Chapter 8 Test Form A

1. 1

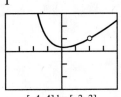

[–4, 4] by [–3, 3]

2. (a)

x	$f(x)$
10	1.5383
10^2	1.7299
10^3	1.7480
10^4	1.7498
10^5	1.7500

    Limit: 1.75

    (b) $\displaystyle\lim_{x\to\infty} f(x) = \lim_{x\to\infty} \frac{14x - 8}{8x}$

         $= \displaystyle\lim_{x\to\infty} \frac{14}{8} = 1.75$

3. $e^{2.5}$

4. L'Hôpital's rule cannot be applied to

    $\displaystyle\lim_{x\to\infty} \frac{\sin(1/x)}{e^{1/x}}$ because it corresponds to $\dfrac{0}{1}$, which
is not an indeterminate form.

5. (B)

6. $(\ln x)^2,\ 3x^5\,x^6,\ e^{2x}$

7. One possible answer:

    $\displaystyle\lim_{x\to\infty} \frac{5^x}{5^{x-3}} = 125$, so f_1 and f_2 grow at the same
    rate. $\displaystyle\lim_{x\to\infty} \frac{5^x + 3^x}{5^x} = \lim_{x\to\infty} \left[1 + \left(\frac{3}{5}\right)^x\right] = 1$, so f_1
    and f_3 grow at the same rate. By transitivity, f_2

    and f_3 grow at the same rate.

8. (E)

9. (a) Diverges   (b) Converges

    (c) Diverges

10. 3   **11.** 3

12. 7   **13.** $\dfrac{3}{x} + \dfrac{4}{x^2} - \dfrac{5}{x+2}$

14. $6 \ln |x - 3| - 2 \ln |x + 4| + C$

15. $\ln |y - 2| - \ln |y| = 2 \sin x - 2 \sin 1$

16. $\dfrac{1}{5}(36 - x^2)^{5/2} - 12(36 - x^2)^{3/2} + C$

Chapter 8 Test Form B

1. -2

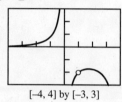

[−4, 4] by [−3, 3]

2. (a)

x	$f(x)$
10	1.9147
10^2	1.6943
10^3	1.6694
10^4	1.6669
10^5	1.6667

Limit: $\dfrac{5}{3}$

(b) $\displaystyle\lim_{x \to \infty} f(x) = \lim_{x \to \infty} \dfrac{10x}{6x - 5}$

$\displaystyle= \lim_{x \to \infty} \dfrac{10}{6} = \dfrac{5}{3}$

3. e^6

4. L'Hôpital's rule cannot be applied to

$\displaystyle\lim_{x \to 0} \dfrac{4x^2 - 5x + 1}{2x^2 + 3x - 5}$ because it corresponds to $-\dfrac{1}{5}$, which is not an indeterminate form.

5. (A)   **6.** $(\ln x)^3$, $4x^2$, e^{2x}, 10^x

7. One possible answer:

$\displaystyle\lim_{x \to \infty} \dfrac{2x^5 + x^2}{x^5} = \lim_{x \to \infty} (2 + x^{-3}) = 2$, so f_1 and f_2 grow at the same rate.

$\displaystyle\lim_{x \to \infty} \dfrac{x^5 + \ln x}{x^5} = \lim_{x \to \infty} \left(1 + \dfrac{\ln x}{x^5}\right) = 1$, so f_1 and f_3 grow at the same rate. By transitivity, f_2 and f_3 grow at the same rate.

8. (B)

9. (a) Diverges   (b) Diverges

    (c) Converges

10. $\dfrac{1}{4}$ **11.** 1

12. 4   **13.** $\dfrac{5}{x} + \dfrac{2}{x - 1} - \dfrac{4}{(x-1)^2}$

14. $3 \ln |x + 5| - 2 \ln |x - 1| + C$

15. $-3 \cos y = \ln |x| - \ln |x + 3| + \ln 4$

16. $\dfrac{49}{\sqrt{49 - x^2}} + \sqrt{49 - x^2} + C$

Chapter 9

Quiz: Sections 9.1–9.3

1. (A)   **2.** (D)

3. (C)   **4.** (A)

5. (C)   **6.** (B)

7. (D)   **8.** (B)

9. (D)

Quiz: Sections 9.4–9.5

1. (C)   **2.** (E)

3. (C)   **4.** (E)

5. (C)   **6.** (B)

7. (C)

Chapter 9 Test Form A

1. $\dfrac{x^2}{5} + \dfrac{x^3}{8} + \dfrac{x^4}{11} + \dfrac{x^5}{14}$ **2.** Converges to $\dfrac{8}{3}$

3. $\displaystyle\sum_{n=0}^{\infty} 0.621(0.001)^n = \dfrac{23}{37}$

4. $x^3 - x^5 + x^7 - \cdots + (-1)^n x^{2n+3} + \cdots$

5. $1 - 2\left(x - \dfrac{\pi}{4}\right)^2$

6. $P_3(x) = 5 - 3x + 4x^2 + 4x^3$; $f(0.4) \approx 4.696$

7. (a) 3

(b) $2x + 3x^2 + 2x^3 + \cdots + \dfrac{(n+1)x^n}{(n-1)!} + \cdots$

(c) $x + x^2 + \dfrac{x^3}{2} + \dfrac{x^4}{6} + \cdots + \dfrac{x^{n+1}}{n!} + \cdots$

8. $P_4(x) = -x^2 - \dfrac{x^4}{2}$; $f(0.3) \approx -0.09405$

9. (a) $\approx 3.642 \times 10^{-5}$ (b) $\approx 3.535 \times 10^{-5}$

10. (C)

11. Tests used may vary.

(a) Diverges by Ratio Test

(b) Converges by Ratio Test.

(c) Diverges by nth-Term Test.

12. (a) Converges absolutely

    (b) Converges conditionally

    (c) Converges absolutely

13. (a) $\dfrac{3}{5}$ **(b)** 3

14. Interval: $\dfrac{1}{4} < x < \dfrac{5}{4}$; Sum: $\dfrac{8}{8 - (4x - 3)^3}$

15. $k\pi - \dfrac{\pi}{6} \le x \le k\pi + \dfrac{\pi}{6}$ for any integer k

16. $\dfrac{4}{3} \le x < \dfrac{8}{3}$ **17. (E)**

Chapter 9 Test Form B

1. $\dfrac{x^3}{5} + \dfrac{x^4}{7} + \dfrac{x^5}{9} + \dfrac{x^6}{11}$ **2.** Converges to 15

3. $\displaystyle\sum_{n=0}^{\infty} 0.516(0.001)^n = \dfrac{172}{333}$

4. $x^5 - \dfrac{x^8}{2} + \dfrac{x^{11}}{3} + \cdots + \dfrac{(-1)^{n-1}x^{3n+2}}{n} + \cdots$

5. $-1 + \dfrac{9}{2}\left(x - \dfrac{\pi}{3}\right)^2$

6. $P_3(x) = 9 + 5x - 2x^2 + 6x^3$;
    $f(0.3) \approx 10.482$

7. (a) 6

    (b) $2x + 6x^2 + 6x^3 + \dfrac{10}{3}x^4 + \cdots$
         $+ \dfrac{n(n+1)x^n}{(n-1)!} + \cdots$

    (c) $x^2 + x^3 + \dfrac{x^4}{2} + \dfrac{x^5}{6} + \cdots + \dfrac{x^{n+1}}{(n-1)!} + \cdots$

8. $P_4(x) = 1 - x^2 + x^4$; $f(0.2) \approx 0.9616$

9. (a) $\approx 1.698 \times 10^{-4}$ **(b)** $\approx 1.624 \times 10^{-4}$

10. (D)

11. Tests used may vary.

    (a) Converges by Ratio Test

    (b) Diverges by nth-Term Test.

    (c) Converges by Direct Comparison with
         $\displaystyle\sum \dfrac{1}{n^2}$.

12. (a) Diverges

    (b) Converges absolutely

    (c) Converges absolutely

13. (a) $\dfrac{7}{4}$ **(b)** $\dfrac{5}{3}$

14. Interval: $\dfrac{1}{2} < x < 2$; Sum: $\dfrac{9}{9 - (4x - 5)^2}$

15. $k\pi - \dfrac{\pi}{3} < x < k\pi + \dfrac{\pi}{3}$ for any integer k

16. $-\dfrac{5}{2} < x \le \dfrac{1}{2}$ **17. (C)**

Chapter 10

Quiz: Sections 10.1–10.3

1. (D)   **2. (B)**

3. (E)   **4. (A)**

5.

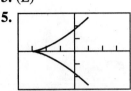

    $[-4, 4]$ by $[-3, 3]$

6. (B)   **7. (C)**

Quiz: Sections 10.4–10.6

1. (D)   **2. (B)**

3.

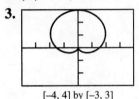

    $[-4, 4]$ by $[-3, 3]$

4. (D)   **5. (E)**

6. (D)   **7. (A)**

Chapter 10 Test Form A

1. $\dfrac{dy}{dx} = \dfrac{e^{2t}}{t}$; $\dfrac{d^2y}{dx^2} = \dfrac{(2t - 1)e^{2t}}{2t^3}$

2. 28   **3.** 9424π

4. (a) $\langle 1, 4 \rangle$ **(b)** $\sqrt{17}$

    (c) -17

5. Tangent: $\left\langle \dfrac{21}{29}, -\dfrac{20}{29} \right\rangle, \left\langle -\dfrac{21}{29}, \dfrac{20}{29} \right\rangle$

    Normal: $\left\langle -\dfrac{20}{29}, -\dfrac{21}{29} \right\rangle, \left\langle \dfrac{20}{29}, \dfrac{21}{29} \right\rangle$

6. ≈ 396.0 mph; $28.5°$ west of north

7. (a)

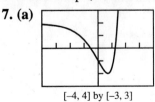

    $[-4, 4]$ by $[-3, 3]$

    (b) $\mathbf{v}(t) = \left(\dfrac{1}{t+2}\right)\mathbf{i} + (2t)\mathbf{j}$;

        $\mathbf{a}(t) = \left(-\dfrac{1}{(t+2)^2}\right)\mathbf{i} + 2\mathbf{j}$

8. $\mathbf{r}(t) = (e^{3t})\mathbf{i} + (t^2 - 4)\mathbf{j}$

9. ≈ 16.14 ft; ≈ 2.01 sec; ≈ 76.94 ft

10. ≈ 6.99 m   **11.** (E)

12.

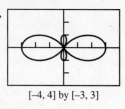

[−4, 4] by [−3, 3]

13. (E)

14. Three possible answers are

$$1 = \frac{\sqrt{x^2 + y^2}}{x^2}; \ x^4 = x^2 + y^2, x \neq 0;$$

and $y = \pm x\sqrt{x^2 - 1}$.

15. At $\dfrac{\pi}{6}$: $\dfrac{\sqrt{3}}{3}$; at $\dfrac{\pi}{3}$: $-\dfrac{\sqrt{3}}{3}$

16. 27π **17.** $10 - 5\sqrt{3}$

Chapter 10 Test Form B

1. $\dfrac{dy}{dx} = \dfrac{t^2}{e^{3t}}; \dfrac{d^2y}{dx^2} = \dfrac{2t - 3t^2}{3e^{6t}}$

2. 48   **3.** $\dfrac{7808\pi}{3}$

4. (a) $\langle -1, 3 \rangle$ (b) $\sqrt{10}$

    (c) -26

5. Tangent: $\left\langle \dfrac{7}{25}, \dfrac{24}{25} \right\rangle, \left\langle -\dfrac{7}{25}, -\dfrac{24}{25} \right\rangle.$

  Normal: $\left\langle \dfrac{24}{25}, -\dfrac{7}{25} \right\rangle, \left\langle -\dfrac{24}{25}, \dfrac{7}{25} \right\rangle$

6. ≈ 347.8 mph; 55.7° east of north
(or 34.3° north of east)

7. (a)

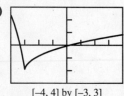

[−4, 4] by [−3, 3]

  (b) $\mathbf{v}(t) = (3t^2)\mathbf{i} + (-2e^{-2t} + 2)\mathbf{j}$;
    $\mathbf{a}(t) = (6t)\mathbf{i} + (4e^{-2t})\mathbf{j}$

8. $\mathbf{r}(t) = (t^3 + 4)\mathbf{i} + \cos(t - 1)\mathbf{j}$

9. ≈ 25.19 ft; ≈ 2.51 sec; ≈ 143.89 ft

10. ≈ 2.49 m   **11.** (C)

12.

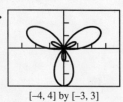

[−4, 4] by [−3, 3]

13. (B)

14. Three possible answers are

$$\frac{\sqrt{x^2 + y^2}}{xy} = 1; \ x^2 + y^2 = x^2y^2, x \neq 0, y \neq 0;$$

and $y = \pm \dfrac{x}{\sqrt{x^2 - 1}}$.

15. At $\dfrac{\pi}{4}$: -1; at $\dfrac{\pi}{3}$: $\sqrt{3}$ **16.** $\dfrac{41\pi}{2}$

17. $3\sqrt{2}$

Final Tests

Final Test Chapters 1–7 Form A

1. (a) ∞ (b) 9
  (c) 1   (d) 4

2. $y = 2x - 5, y = 18x - 85$

3. $4x^3 - 15x^2 + 2$

4. $\dfrac{2x \cos x + (x^2 - 5) \sin x}{\cos^2 x}$

5. $\dfrac{6xy - 10x + 1}{3y^2 - 3x^2}$

6. (E)

7.

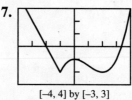

[−4, 4] by [−3, 3]

8. (a) $(-\infty, -1.477]$ and $[-0.172, \infty)$
  (b) $[-1.477, -0.172]$
  (c) $(-0.707, 0.707)$
  (d) $(-\infty, -0.707)$ and $(0.707, \infty)$
  (e) Min: -3.085 at $x \approx -0.172$;
    max: -1.816 at $x \approx -1.477$
  (f) $(-0.707, -2.527), (0.707, -1.112)$

9. (a) $f' = 0$: $x = -1, x = 1, x = 3$;
    $f' > 0$: $-1 < x < 1, x > 3$;
    $f' < 0$: $x < -1, 1 < x < 3$
  (b) $f'' = 0$: $x = 0, x = 2$;
    $f'' > 0$: $x < 0, x > 2$
    $f'' < 0$: $0 < x < 2$

10. (a) $12 - \sqrt{39} \approx 5.755$ in.
  (b) ≈ 3244.4 in^3

11. (E)   **12.** $x_2 \approx 19.379$

13. (a) -80 ft^3/sec   (b) -4 ft^2/sec
  (c) $\dfrac{25}{3\sqrt{21}} \approx 1.818$ ft/sec

14. 180 ft

15. $\int_7^{15} \left(2x + \dfrac{1}{x^2}\right) dx$

16. (a) 20   **(b)** 18

    (c) $\dfrac{52}{3}$

17. (a) 7   **(b)** 5

    (c) -5

18. $\dfrac{3\pi}{4} + 2$ **19.** ≈ 7.498

20. $10 - 4x$

21. (a) -4 **(b)** $\dfrac{508}{7}$

    (c) -1

22. (D)   **23.** ≈ 19.482

24. (B)

25. $\dfrac{1}{5}x^5 + \dfrac{4}{x} + \dfrac{1}{2}e^{2x} + C$

26. $y = \dfrac{1}{12}(3x - 4)^4 - \dfrac{13}{12}$

27.

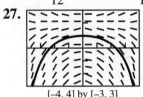

[−4, 4] by [−3, 3]

28. $\dfrac{2}{7}\sqrt{\tan^7 x} + C$

29. $\dfrac{1}{2}\sin(x^2) = \dfrac{1}{3}y^3 - 2y + C$

30. $-\dfrac{x}{2}\cos(2x - 5) + \dfrac{1}{4}\sin(2x - 5) + C$

31. $\left(-\dfrac{1}{2}x^3 - \dfrac{3}{4}x^2 - \dfrac{3}{4}x - \dfrac{3}{8}\right)e^{-2x} + C$

32. ≈ 104.48 g

33. (a) $y = \dfrac{800.369}{1 + 4.250e^{-0.12043x}}$

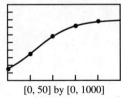

[0, 50] by [0, 1000]

    (b) ≈ 800 deer

    (c) Year: 1962; population: ≈ 400

34. (a) Right: $2 < t \le 8$, left: $0 \le t < 2$; stopped: $t = 2$

    (b) 32 ft   **(c)** 40 ft

35. 879.84 gal   **36.** $\dfrac{45}{4}$

37. (D)   **38.** $\dfrac{117\pi}{5}$

39. $\dfrac{\sqrt{3}}{2}$ **40.** $\dfrac{62}{3}$

41. 720 N-cm

Final Test Chapters 1–7 Form B

1. (a) 6   **(b)** -2

    (c) 1   **(d)** $-\infty$

2. $y = 4x - 10, \ y = 12x - 42$

3. $6x^5 + 16x - 11$

4. $\dfrac{(x^2 + 3)\cos x - 2x \sin x}{x^4 + 6x^2 + 9}$

5. $\dfrac{12x^2 y - 1}{15y^2 - 4x^3 - 8}$

6. (D)

7.

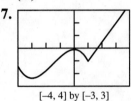

[−4, 4] by [−3, 3]

8. (a) $(-\infty, -1.393]$ and $[-0.209, \infty)$

    (b) $[-1.393, -0.209]$

    (c) $(-0.707, 0.707)$

    (d) $(-\infty, -0.707)$ and $(0.707, \infty)$

    (e) Min: -5.204 at $x \approx -0.209$; Max: -3.504 at $x \approx -1.393$

    (f) $(-0.707, -4.447), (0.707, -1.618)$

9. (a) $f' = 0: x = -3, x = -1, x = 1$; $f' > 0: x < -3, -1 < x < 1$; $f' < 0: -3 < x < -1, x > 1$

    (b) $f'' = 0: x = -2, x = 0$; $f'' > 0: -2 < x < 0$ $f'' < 0: x < -2, x > 0$

10. (a) $\dfrac{28}{3} - \dfrac{4}{3}\sqrt{13} \approx 4.526$ in.

    (b) ≈ 1552.5 in^3

11. (B)   **12.** $x_2 \approx 0.736$

13. (a) -243 ft^3/sec   **(b)** -108 ft^2/sec

    (c) $-\dfrac{6}{\sqrt{146}} \approx -0.497$ ft/sec

14. 930 ft

15. $\int_3^{11} \left(5x^2 - \dfrac{3}{x}\right) dx$

16. (a) 30   **(b)** $\dfrac{95}{2}$

    (c) $\dfrac{140}{3}$

17. (a) -4 **(b)** -1

    (c) -67

18. $5 - \pi$ **19.** ≈ 4.985

20. $18x - 21$

21. (a) 186 **(b)** $\dfrac{93}{5}$

   (c) $\dfrac{2}{\sqrt{3}} \approx 1.155$

22. (E) **23.** ≈ 10.783

24. (E)

25. $\dfrac{1}{2}x^6 + \dfrac{1}{2x^2} + \dfrac{1}{7}e^{7x} + C$

26. $y = -\dfrac{1}{15}(-5x + 7)^3 - \dfrac{7}{15}$

27.

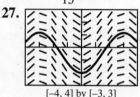

[−4, 4] by [−3, 3]

28. $\dfrac{1}{5}\sec^5 x + C$

29. $\dfrac{1}{2}x^2 + 7x = -\cos(y^3) + C$

30. $\dfrac{x}{3}\sin(3x + 4) + \dfrac{1}{9}\cos(3x + 4) + C$

31. $\left(-\dfrac{1}{5}x^2 - \dfrac{2}{25}x - \dfrac{2}{125}\right)e^{-5x} + C$

32. ≈ 120.39 g

33. (a) $y = \dfrac{666.731}{1 + 28.432e^{-0.16462x}}$

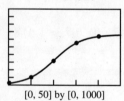

[0, 50] by [0, 1000]

   (b) ≈ 667 coyotes

   (c) Year: 1970; population: 333

34. (a) Right: $0 \le t < 3$; left: $3 < t \le 10$;
   stopped: $t = 3$

   (b) -60 ft **(c)** 87 ft

35. 2187.5 gal **36.** $\dfrac{27}{2}$

37. (C) **38.** $\dfrac{625\pi}{3}$

39. $\dfrac{2}{5}$ **40.** $\dfrac{1022}{27}$

41. 144 N-cm

Final Test Chapters 1–10 Form A

1. (a) ∞ **(b)** 9

   (c) 1 **(d)** 4

2. $y = 2x - 5$, $y = 18x - 85$

3. $\dfrac{2x\cos x + (x^2 - 5)\sin x}{\cos^2 x}$

4. $\dfrac{6xy - 10x + 1}{3y^2 - 3x^2}$

5. (E)

6. (a) $(-\infty, -1.477]$ and $[-0.172, \infty)$

   (b) $[-1.477, -0.172]$

   (c) $(-0.707, 0.707)$

   (d) $(-\infty, -0.707)$ and $(0.707, \infty)$

   (e) Min: -3.085 at $x \approx -0.172$;
   max: -1.816 at $x \approx -1.477$

   (f) $(-0.707, -2.527)$, $(0.707, -1.112)$

7. (a) $12 - \sqrt{39} \approx 5.755$ in.

   (b) ≈ 3244.4 in^3

8. (a) 20 **(b)** 18

   (c) $\dfrac{52}{3}$

9. $10 - 4x$ **10.** (B)

11. $y = \dfrac{1}{12}(3x - 4)^4 - \dfrac{13}{12}$

12. $\dfrac{1}{2}\sin(x^2) = \dfrac{1}{3}y^3 - 2y + C$

13. $-\dfrac{x}{2}\cos(2x - 5) + \dfrac{1}{4}\sin(2x - 5) + C$

14. ≈ 104.48 g

15. (a) $y = \dfrac{800.369}{1 + 4.250e^{-0.12043x}}$

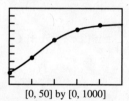

[0, 50] by [0, 1000]

   (b) ≈ 800 deer

   (c) Year: 1962; population: ≈ 400

16.

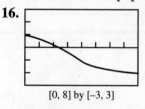

[0, 8] by [−3, 3]

17. (a) Right: $2 < t \le 8$, left: $0 \le t < 2$;
   stopped: $t = 2$

   (b) 32 ft **(c)** 40 ft

18. $\dfrac{45}{4}$ **19.** (D)

20. $\dfrac{117\pi}{5}$ **21.** $\dfrac{62}{3}$

22. 720 N-cm

23. (a) $\dfrac{5}{4}$ **(b)** $e^{1.2} \approx 3.32$

24. $\ln(x+3), 5x^2, x^3\, e^{x/2}$

25. $\dfrac{1}{3(\ln 2)^3} \approx 1.001$ **26. (A)**

27. $2x^2 + 16x + 3\ln|x+1| + 12\ln|x-5| + C$

28. Converges to $\dfrac{20}{7}$

29. $x + 2x^2 + 2x^3 + \cdots + \dfrac{2^n x^{n+1}}{n!} + \cdots$

30. ≈ 36.6

31. One possible answer:

Converges by Direct Comparison with

$$\sum_{n=1}^{\infty} \dfrac{1}{n^2}.$$

32. (D)   **33.** $1 \le x < 5$

34. (B)   **35.** $12\pi^2 + 8\pi$

36. (a) $\langle 6, -31 \rangle$ **(b)** $\sqrt{53}$
   (c) 11

37. $\mathbf{r} = (2e^{t/2} - 5t - 2)\mathbf{i} + \left(\dfrac{2}{5}(t+4)^{5/2} - \dfrac{29}{5}\right)\mathbf{j}$

38. ≈ 22.415 ft/sec

39. (a)

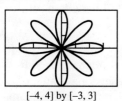

[−4, 4] by [−3, 3]

   (b) 2π

40. $5\sqrt{3} - \dfrac{5\pi}{3}$

Final Test Chapters 1–10 Form B

1. (a) 6   **(b)** −2
   (c) 1   **(d)** $-\infty$

2. $y = 4x - 10, y = 12x - 42$

3. $\dfrac{(x^2 + 3)\cos x - 2x\sin x}{x^4 + 6x^2 + 9}$

4. $\dfrac{12x^2 y - 1}{15y^2 - 4x^3 - 8}$

5. (D)

6. (a) $(-\infty, -1.393]$ and $[-0.209, \infty)$
   (b) $[-1.393, -0.209]$
   (c) $(-0.707, 0.707)$
   (d) $(-\infty, -0.707)$ and $(0.707, \infty)$
   (e) Min: -5.204 at $x \approx -0.209$;
       Max: -3.504 at $x \approx -1.393$
   (f) $(-0.707, -4.447), (0.707, -1.618)$

7. (a) $\dfrac{28}{3} - \dfrac{4}{3}\sqrt{13} \approx 4.526$ in.
   (b) ≈ 1552.5 in^3

8. (a) 30   **(b)** $\dfrac{95}{2}$
   (c) $\dfrac{140}{3}$

9. $18x - 21$ **10. (E)**

11. $y = -\dfrac{1}{15}(-5x + 7)^3 - \dfrac{7}{15}$

12. $\dfrac{1}{2}x^2 + 7x = -\cos(y^3) + C$

13. $\dfrac{x}{3}\sin(3x + 4) + \dfrac{1}{9}\cos(3x + 4) + C$

14. ≈ 120.39 g

15. (a) $y = \dfrac{666.731}{1 + 28.432e^{-0.16462x}}$

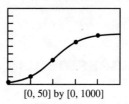

[0, 50] by [0, 1000]

   (b) ≈ 667 coyotes
   (c) Year: 1970; population: 333

16.

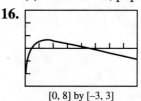

[0, 8] by [−3, 3]

17. (a) Right: $0 \le t < 3$; left: $3 < t \le 10$;
       stopped: $t = 3$
   (b) -60 ft   **(c)** 87 ft

18. $\dfrac{27}{2}$ **19. (C)**

20. $\dfrac{625\pi}{3}$ **21.** $\dfrac{1022}{27}$

22. 144 N-cm

23. (a) $-\dfrac{14}{3}$ **(b)** $e^{-6} \approx 0.00248$

24. $\ln(5x), (x+2)^3, x^4, e^{x/3}$

25. $2\sqrt{\ln 5} \approx 2.537$ **26. (D)**

27. $2x^2 + 3x + 6\ln|x+2| + 21\ln|x-3| + C$

28. Converges to $\dfrac{5}{2}$

29. $3 - \dfrac{9}{2}x + 9x^2 - \cdots + (-1)^n \dfrac{3^{n+1}x^n}{n+1} + \cdots$

30. ≈ 89.4

31. One possible answer:
   Converges by Ratio Test.

32. (B)   **33.** $\dfrac{5}{3} < x \le \dfrac{7}{3}$

34. (D)   **35.** $30\pi^2 + 18\pi$

36. (a) $\langle 31, 18 \rangle$ **(b)** $\sqrt{29}$

  (c) -8

37. $\mathbf{r} = \left(\dfrac{2}{3}(t+9)^{3/2} - 13\right)\mathbf{i} + \left(\dfrac{1}{2}e^{2t} + t^2 - \dfrac{1}{2}\right)\mathbf{j}$

38. ≈ 19.258 ft/sec

39. (a)

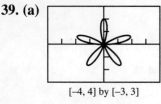

[−4, 4] by [−3, 3]

  (b) π

40. $\dfrac{9\sqrt{3}}{2} - \dfrac{3\pi}{2}$

Alternative Assessment
Chapter 1

Group Activity

Use the identities $\sec^{-1} x = \cos^{-1}\left(\dfrac{1}{x}\right)$,

$\csc^{-1} x = \sin^{-1}\left(\dfrac{1}{x}\right)$, and $\cot^{-1} x = \dfrac{\pi}{2} - \tan^{-1} x$

Student Log (or Journal)

If f is not one-to-one, then there are values a and b for which $f(a) = f(b)$, so $f^{-1}(f(a))$ is not uniquely determined. Thus, the inverse relation for f is not a function.

Discussion Questions

Inaccurate predictions can occur if the wrong kind of regression is used or if the pattern seen in the known data does not continue.

Chapter 2

Group Activity

If $f(x)$ is continuous at $x = a$, $\lim\limits_{x \to a} f(x)$ can be determined by simply evaluating $f(a)$.

Limits as x approaches infinity are useful in

determining the long-run behavior of functions.

Student Log (or Journal)

A graphing utility does not always show discontinuities and can be misleading if a function is slow to rise or fall to its limit.

Discussion Questions

The limit to infinity can show long-run behavior of the company or the limit to how much revenue or profit will be made by greatly increasing output.

Chapter 3

Group Activity

For e^x and its multiples, the function and its derivative are the same. The exponential function is simple in the sense that the derivative of $f(x) = e^{nx}$ is the same as $f(x)$ multiplied by n.

Student Log (or Journal)

The graphs show the derivative of y_1 to be equal to y_2 which shows the effect of the chain rule.

Discussion Questions

Implicit differentiation can often be used to find slopes of curves when these slopes cannot be determined using other methods. Also, results obtained by implicit differentiation are often simpler than those obtained by other methods since the results can be given in terms of x and y instead of having to list different expression for different "pieces" of the curve.

Chapter 4

Group Activity

The constant shifts the antiderivative vertically.

Student Log (or Journal)

The second derivative test can show periods where costs or revenues will be increasing or decreasing even if they are still rising.

Discussion Questions

Linearizations are often much simpler than the original function. They are especially useful in examining the behavior of a complicated function over a small interval.

Chapter 5

Group Activity

The Trapezoidal Rule will give an overestimate, and MRAM will give an underestimate.

Student Log (or Journal)

They are different if $f(x) < 0$ for some values of x between a and b, or if $b < a$.

Discussion Questions

NINT can be used when a function is too complicated to antidifferentiate, and it is also useful for verifying results found analytically. It is important to be able to solve integrals analytically because this method gives exact results.

Chapter 6

Group Activity

If d = coasting distance, then $k = \dfrac{v_0 m}{d}$ and the distance function is

$s(t) = \dfrac{v_0 m}{k}(1 - e^{-(k/m)t}) = d(1 - e^{-(v_0/d)t})$, so the distance function can be determined from v_0 and d alone.

Student Log (or Journal)

The expression for u should become simpler when differentiated, and dv should remain manageable when integrated. Usually, the "LIPET method" (logarithm, inverse trigonometric function, polynomial, exponential function, trigonometric function) can be used to find u.

Discussion Questions

The improved method uses averaging. The expression $f(x_{n-1}, y_{n-1}) + f(x_n, z_n)$ is a better estimate than $f(x_{n-1}, y_{n-1})$ for the average slope of the solution curve from x_{n-1} to x_n.

Chapter 7

Group Activity

Only in very few cases would the areas or volumes be equal.

Student Log (or Journal)

Integrals can give the exact volume of curved regions and can be used to derive general formulas for volume, such as for spheres and cones.

Discussion Questions

The center of mass is important because of moving object's position and movement can be described as if the object were only a particle located at the object's center of mass.

Chapter 8

Group Activity

The calculation is incorrect. The integral diverges because $\int_{-2}^{0} \dfrac{dx}{x}$ diverges and $\int_{0}^{2} \dfrac{dx}{x}$ diverges.

Student Log (or Journal)

L'Hôpital's rule is important because it is very simple and can be used to find limits of indeterminate forms which may appear to be impossible to evaluate otherwise. The danger of l'Hôpital's rule is that if one attempts to apply it to an expression which is not an indeterminate form, the results will not be reliable.

Discussion Questions

The intensity I increases by $20n$. We might say that the intensity I grows slower than the pressure P.

Chapter 9

Group Activity

For sin x (with $x > 0$) and for cos x (with $x \neq 0$), each Taylor polynomial with an odd number of nonzero terms overestimates, and each Taylor polynomial with an even number of terms underestimates. For sin x (with $x < 0$), the reverse is true. (Note that this is the expected behavior based on our study of alternating series.)

Student Log (or Journal)

No, the Remainder Estimation Theorem gives a *bound* on the error, not the actual error, and only when f satisfies the appropriate conditions.

Discussion Questions

Simply replace x by $-x$ in the formula and simplify the series.

Chapter 10

Group Activity

For different values of m, the period of the curve changes. Different values of n expand or contract the curves and switching sin and cos changes the direction.

Student Log (or Journal)

Polar coordinates greatly simplify equations for cardioids and the like and can also be used to graph conic sections without having to enter separate equations for the upper and lower portion of the graph.

Discussion Questions

The student is incorrect. $(2\pi, 0)$ and $(-2\pi, -\pi)$ are both equivalent to $(-2\pi, \pi)$, which does satisfy the equation.

© Addison Wesley Longman, Inc.